THE BIOGRAPHY OF FIELD MARSHAL ERWIN
ROMMEL

THE BIOGRAPHY OF FIELD MARSHAL ERWIN
ROMMEL

WARD RUTHERFORD

Book Value International.
NORTHBROOK, ILLINOIS

A Bison Book

CONTENTS

1: A STATE FUNERAL

The body of the murdered field marshal was laid in state in the Town Hall of Ulm not far from where he had been born and brought up. At its feet were the ensignia of his rank: his field marshal's baton, sword and helmet and with them, sparkling on a cushion, the decorations won in two world wars.

At each of the four corners of the catafalque stood officers wearing the armband of the Afrika Korps with its palmtree insignia, but just before the funeral service started, they were replaced by four generals of the Wehrmacht. Outside, in the bleak October weather, companies of infantry, Luftwaffe and the Waffen-SS paraded.

Another field marshal, Gerd von Rundstedt, senior serving officer of the German army, entered the hall with Rommel's widow and son. As they did so, the band struck up Hitler's favorite funeral march, from Wagner's *Götterdamerung.* Tall and dignified, von Rundstedt was well cast in his role as the Führer's personal representative. He was to place the leader's extravagantly huge wreath before the coffin and also to deliver the eulogy.

Inevitably this dwelt on the dead soldier's great military skill; his victories in North Africa; how later he had worked tirelessly to try to make Western Europe impregnable to an Allied invasion; how, through his career, he had been a fighter for the Reich, imbued with the National Socialist spirit, finally dying with the Führer still in his heart.

That the funeral should have been at Ulm was to complete the cycle of the dead man's life with uncanny symmetry. He was born only a few miles away at Heidenheim on the River Brenz on 15 November 1891 and in due course christened Erwin Johannes Eugen. His father, Professor Erwin Rommel, was a local schoolmaster and like his own father something of a mathematician with a renown beyond his own locality.

The young Erwin was the second son born to the family. The first, Manfred, died in infancy so that Erwin took on the burdens of being the eldest child. He was conservative, self-confident, first emulating, then seeking to outstrip his father, quick to mature and enjoying responsibility. In fact, these qualities were to serve him well when his father died in 1913 after an operation and, at

Left: Rommel's coffin is carried from the Town Hall at Ulm.
Below: Field Marshal von Rundstedt delivers the oration at Rommel's funeral. The speech was almost certainly composed by Goebbel's Propaganda Ministry.

22, Rommel became head of a household which included two brothers and a sister, Helene. He also demonstrated another characteristic of the elder son thus bereaved – that of needing a father-figure, which in due time he was to find.

From an unpromising start at school where he was the sort of dreamy child of whom teachers write 'could do better,' in adolescence he seemed to undergo a metamorphosis. He developed a taste for sport and the outdoors, cycling and tennis in summer, skiing in winter. He began to show an inherited gift for mathematics. When his younger brother, Karl, joined the army to avoid taking difficult school examinations, Erwin stayed on and passed his with ease. He had become hard-headed, practical, down to earth. His birthplace, Heidenheim and Aalen where the family moved after his father became director of its *Realschule* in 1898 are both in the *Land* of Baden-Württemberg and the Württembergers pride themselves on their

common sense. Thus, the young Rommel was turning into a true son of his *Land*. He became interested in aeronautics. At 14, he and a friend named Keitel built a glider which, from an existing picture looks very like a box-kite. This he claimed flew, 'though not very far.' Keitel was to follow his bent and become an engineer in the Zeppelin factory at Friedrichshaven. Rommel would have liked to follow him there, but his parents objected and it was apparently as a result of this that he decided to go into the army in which his father had served briefly as a lieutenant of artillery.

He first applied to join his father's old regiment and, when rejected, turned equally unsuccessfully to the engineers. However, in the spring of 1910 he was ordered to report to the 124th Württemberg Regimental headquarters for medical examination. He was accepted despite the discovery of a slight malfunction of a toe bone which was corrected by an

operation.

On 19 July, at the age of 18, he joined his regiment at Weingarten, doing the mandatory period in the ranks for eight months, during which he was promoted to corporal and then sergeant.

The following March he was sent to the Royal Officer Cadet Academy at Danzig. There is little evidence that he indulged with any passion in the cadet pastimes of gambling, drinking and wenching. It may, however, have been at this time that he developed his taste for the chase, the only recreation he was to pursue with anything approximating enthusiasm in later life. Otherwise, his conduct was distinguished by an Appolonian moderation. Perhaps because he found formal study difficult, he spent a disproportionate amount of his time closeted with his books. Often he was

Below: The carefully orchestrated funeral ceremonial continues. Many in the crowd give Nazi salutes as the procession begins.

Above: Count von Schlieffen devised the strategic plan used by the German Army in 1914.

doing so while others were out socializing and it was a sign of his good nature that he was usually prepared to undertake their duties for them, though they soon found he was not a young man to be put upon.

His sole concession to the image of the German officer of the time was an attempt to grow a moustache which failed because he was too fair and the sporting of a monocle which, being forbidden to cadets, had to be done in secret. It was one of the few examples we have of Rommel's ever deviating from the rules as laid down by authority.

Very early in his stay in Danzig he met Lucie Maria Mollin, the cousin of a fellow cadet and herself the daughter of a local landowner. She was dark, pretty, vivacious and crazy about dancing. In the custom of the time their romance was conducted with maximum propriety, the young couple never meeting save in the presence of a third party.

It thrived, all the same, and though there was no formal betrothal and it was to be four years before they married, Rommel behaved thereafter as a man affianced. When he returned to his regimental headquarters at Weingarten in 1912, now a second lieutenant, he began the lifelong habit of writing to her daily and showed even less interest in joining in his comrades' nighttime pursuits.

They regarded him as serious and quiet, any tendency to priggishness his rigid conduct might have inspired being compensated for by his well-developed sense of humor. Among his superiors it

was observed that he was good at handling men and that while liked and respected by NCOs – no small achievement for a young subaltern – he stood no nonsense. His manifest abilities were soon put to use by making him responsible for recruit training. Perhaps it was heredity, but there was always something of the schoolmaster in his nature. It expressed itself not only in his setting an example of temperance in smoking, drinking and sex, but also in his aptitude for aphorisms and his tendency to indulge in little lectures even on the battlefield. Nowhere is this better exemplified than in his book *Infanterie Greifft An* (in English as *Infantry Attacks*). Here he describes 13 engagements in which he was personally involved, ending each section with a passage headed Observations in which he draws conclusions and points out lessons. These have an inescapably pedantic ring about them. Thus: 'The attack on the engineer company resting at the head of the main body of troops teaches us that all units of a group must provide for their own security'; 'In a man-to-man fight, the winner is he who has one more round in his magazine'; 'Reconnaissance must be active while the troops are resting.'

In March 1914 Rommel was attached to the 49th Field Artillery Regiment stationed at Ulm. The previous six years had witnessed a gradual increase in European tension, but during the spring and early summer of 1914 there seemed

to be a welcome spirit of conciliation abroad. A typical manifestation of this had come in May of that year when the widened Kiel Canal had been opened for traffic by Kaiser Wilhelm II. Anxious to make it a truly international occasion, the German Admiralty had gone so far as to exclude any vessel of their own named after generals of the Franco–Prussian War in a successful effort to gain French naval participation. The program of naval reviews, regattas, sumptuous balls and receptions combined to herald in what looked like a new era in European relations. When President Raymond Poincaré of France paid a state visit to the Russian Czar, Nicholas II, in July the two men could well assure one another that such points of friction as existed between the major powers would all be amenable to negotiated solutions.

They refused to believe that the one dark cloud on the horizon – the murder in Sarajevo of the heir apparent to the Austro–Hungarian crown – was an event such as might lead to conflict. It was a view shared by most Europeans, which included the young officers of the German Imperial Army, however much they longed for the chance of glory.

Through July, however, the situation gradually deteriorated. Austria demand-

Below: Archduke Franz Ferdinand arrives in Sarajevo on the day of his assassination. He was killed by a young Serbian named Gavrilo Princip.

ed the right to cross into Serbia to pursue and destroy the organization which had provided the killers. Russia, as traditional champion of the Slavs supported its tiny neighbor, while Germany backed Austria because of treaty obligations. With this support Austria increased its demands and, on 28 July, despite a Russian threat to go to war over the issue, its artillery began shelling Sofia.

Germany responded with a warning of its own to Russia. But the Czar was

Right: German troops are given flowers by delighted civilians as they march off to war in 1914.
Below: French troops pictured during the fighting in Lorraine early in the war. Note the rudimentary trench and the old-fashioned uniforms and képis, soon to be replaced.

bound to France in a treaty of mutual defense specifically aimed against the Kaiser's ambitions. Under this an attack on the one would be regarded as an attack upon the other. Britain, in its turn, was joined to both France and Russia through the informal bond of the Triple Entente, while it had also guaranteed the neutrality of Belgium about to be invaded by the Germans.

On 31 July, returning from a ride, Rommel found orders for him to rejoin his regiment. On the next day, 1 August, came the declarations of war.

In the next few days Rommel's regiment was fitted out for combat, and the new field-gray uniforms were issued. Rommel describes these early days of the struggle in *Infantry Attacks* indulging in the emotional prose so often found in

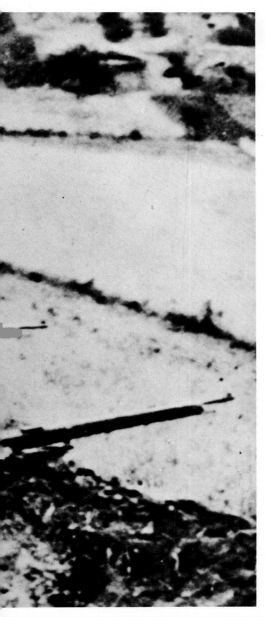

German military writing. Back with his 7th Company of the Württemberg Regiment, he found 'young faces' (he was himself a veteran of 23) which 'radiated joy, animation and anticipation.' That day after a speech from their colonel, mobilization orders arrived. Rommel recalls 'the shouts of German youth eager for battle, rang through the ancient gray cloister buildings.'

By the next day, the regiment was on the move first toward Ravensburg and then Belgium. Everywhere in Germany the regiment was greeted by cheering crowds showering the troops with fruit, chocolate and rolls. Rommel implies in his account that it was the Belgians who were menacing his own country. 'An unending stream of troop trains rolled westward toward the threatened frontier,' he writes.

Desmond Young, one of Rommel's biographers, suggests such passages might have been the interpolations of Nazi propagandists. There is no reason to suppose this is so. For one thing he would have been unlikely to tolerate such tampering. In both style and content it is wholly of a piece with innumerable military memoirs of the time and there is nothing to suggest any hand other than that of the Heidenheim schoolmaster's son was involved.

It was three weeks before Rommel saw action, but in the predawn hours of 22 August, while on a patrol, he ran into enemy forces in the village of Bleid near Longwy. In fog, his platoon had lost contact with the rest of the battalion.

Above: German troops in a small French town on 20 August 1914. The scene in Bleid two days later would have been similar.

They had been on the move for 24 hours and as well as being exhausted, Rommel was himself suffering from an upset stomach, though he had refused to report sick for fear of being regarded as a shirker. The subsequent action is described in detail in *Infantry Attacks* with the usual analysis at the end.

Bleid was covered in a thick fog, but his platoon was halted at the approaches to the village by intense enemy fire. Taking only a sergeant and two other men, Rommel advanced cautiously toward the village. On his own, he succeeded in crawling forward undetected as far as the main street and there saw some 20 French soldiers standing in idle conversation and sipping cups of coffee. Rather than risk losing so vulnerable a target by mustering the whole platoon, he quietly gathered his three men and exploiting the element of surprise rushed the street, all of them firing as they came. When the brief battle ended, 10 Frenchmen lay dead and the rest had taken cover in a farm building. By this time the rest of the platoon, advancing to the sound of fire in the best German military tradition, were coming up. Half were positioned to give covering fire, the rest, armed with timbers and torches of blazing straw, advanced to the farm building and, smashing the door, set it afire with their torches. The farmhouse ablaze, the platoon next began clearing

Left: In the early stages of the war the French took very heavy casualties because of an unrealistic belief in attacking tactics.

the rest of the village, pushing the foe before it.

The struggle went on for several hours with the French troops resisting tenaciously wherever they could find cover, so that what had begun as only a patrol skirmish developed into a small-scale setpiece battle. At its height, Rommel himself, tired, hungry and still sick, collapsed and lost consciousness.

Left: In the early stages of the war the French took very heavy casualties because of an unrealistic belief in attacking tactics.

It was to be some weeks before he fully recovered and there were other fainting spells. He still refused to report sick. However, on 24 September he was forced into hospital when he was wounded in the thigh near Varennes. After nearly three months in hospital he rejoined his regiment. Meanwhile, he had been recommended for the Iron Cross Class II.

During his absence the character of the struggle had entirely changed. The Anglo-French armies, by defeating the Germans at the First Battle of the Marne, had succeeded in dislocating the invaders' grandiose plan for the speedy envelopment and destruction of the Allied forces. The two sides eyed each other across trenchlines defended with barbed wire and machine guns which soon extended from the Swiss frontier to the sea.

Rommel found himself in the Argonne. In the dying days of January 1915, after

another action against the French, he was awarded the Iron Cross, Class I. With his platoon he had made a 100-yard crawl under enemy wire to reach their main position, capturing four French blockhouses and even recapturing one seized by a counterattack, before withdrawing to his own lines with the loss of only six men.

In his analysis of the Argonne action,

Above: German troops training for gas warfare, pictured later in the war when the 'coal-scuttle' helmet had replaced the pickelhaube.
Below: British cavalry advance after the Allied success in the Battle of the Marne.

Rommel claims the reason his men were forced to withdraw was because of a combination of a lack of adequate reserve and a shortage of ammunition. Blaming outside factors for his own misfortunes was a trait which was to become familiar to those close to him.

At the same time he criticized himself for failing to realize that his unit should be equipped with heavy entrenching tools. The ground was frozen hard and the infantrymen's light spades made no impression upon it. He frequently returns to the need to 'dig in,' knowing like the officers of every army that, of all tasks, this is the one most detested by the average soldier. 'Sweat saves blood,' he commented aphoristically after the Meuse attacks of late August 1914. Again, after the Argonne battle: 'Even in the attack, the spade is as important as the rifle.'

A second leg wound, this time from shrapnel saw him back in hospital in July 1915. He hoped, upon recovery, to be sent to the Turkish theater where

Below: German stormtroopers advance. Such units were trained, like Rommel's mountain troops, to work independently in an attack.

early in 1915 the Anglo-French forces had embarked on their calamitous Gallipoli campaign and he even began studying the language. It was in vain. During his sojourn in hospital elements of his regiment had been converted into a Württemberger Mountain Battalion to which Rommel, now a full lieutenant, was posted in October 1915.

Above: German troops rest before the Isonzo attack in Italy in 1917. The attack forced the Italians back 60 miles in two weeks.

The battalion consisted of six rifle companies and an equal number of mountain machine-gun platoons and so was somewhat larger than the normal five-company battalion. In fact, it never

fought as an entity, but always in detachments of varying size, each under its own commander. These men – of whom he was now one – were allowed considerable freedom of action. This must have been congenial.

After a long intensive period of training in Austria they were first sent to the Vosges, but in late August 1916 Rumania made an ill-advised declaration of war on Austria and Germany in return for the promise of considerable territorial spoils after victory. The Württemberger Mountain Battalion was therefore railed east to meet the new threat, joining the *Alpenkorps* already there.

The appointment to the mountain battalion was an important step in his

Above: German machine-gun troops training in Italy. They use captured British Lewis guns, a comparatively light burden in attack.

military career, showing, inter alia, that Rommel's superiors had fully appreciated the independent cast of his mind. However, a no less important one had taken place in his personal life. Before

going to the Rumanian front he was given leave, went to Danzig and there, on 27 November 1916, married Lucie Mollin.

He had shown a remarkable eye for terrain on the plains of France. Now he was to gain a legendary reputation. Mountaineering is challenging enough when all the climber has to worry about is himself and his pack. When on top of this he has his rifle and may have to help haul weapons such as machine guns, mortars and even artillery pieces and still has the enemy to cope with, the task becomes nearly superhuman – hence the renown mountain troops enjoy in every nation which possesses them. Yet Rommel and his men not only did all this but repeatedly achieved surprise and, through surprise, victory.

It became the accepted tactics for his troops to work their way round behind the enemy by way of the upper slopes, which entailed extra climbing. The demands made upon them were the measure of the esteem in which they held their commander and of the confidence he was able to instil. As one old comrade put it, he exerted a spell such as seemed to turn those who came under it into soldiers immediately. Possessed of inexhaustible energy himself, he seemed to have the talent for galvanizing others. He was always in the forefront of danger, taking the greatest risks, before inviting others to follow.

In January 1917 he and his men seized a village by slipping between the outposts, then lying for hours hidden on freezing ground until long after dark when he judged the enemy would be sleeping. With shouts and guns firing, his men burst into the village. Four hundred prisoners were taken, while his own casualties were only slight.

In August 1917 he personally led four companies up a steep track between opposing positions, his signaller laying telephone cables as they went. Wounded in the arm by a bullet, he still went on, going without sleep for a week. The result of the action was the capture of heavily fortified positions on Mount Cosna.

These operations, like the very first one at Bleid in 1914, and in the Argonne in 1915, all bore the same characteristics of a Rommel attack: the stealthy and patient approach to get as close as possible to the main enemy formation and

then the sudden emergence with blazing guns. Already he was manifesting that skill in psychological warfare he was to develop to such a degree. They were tactics much admired by the British, bringing to mind such actions as Francis Drake's daring assault on the assembling Spanish fleet at Cadiz or the commando actions of World War II. We know, too, that Rommel, while deploring what he saw as the often wanton brutality of the British Commandos also admired them.

Where frontal attack was the only possible course, he developed his own methods. In essence, he used narrow as opposed to broad front attacks and it is

Below: German troops cross the Piave. Rommel won the *Pour le Mérite* for his part in the action at Longarone nearby.

not uninteresting that his greatest rival, Bernard Montgomery, was also an advocate of the concentrated, narrow front, attack when it was necessary to hit the enemy frontally. In the smaller-scale actions in which Rommel and his mountaineers were involved the attack would begin with intense machine gun fire along a wide sector with concentration at the intended point of assault. He would then burst through, emplacing machine guns for covering enfilade fire at both lips of the gap.

Having penetrated, the main force pushed on under its own impetus without consideration for what was happening to their rear. It was, one could say, an early employment of Sir Basil Liddell Hart's theory of the 'expanding torrent.' The great apostle of such attacks compared them with a great body of water pouring through a gap in a sea-wall. However slight the initial penetration, sheer momentum will force it through widening the breach and spreading out behind it. It is therefore hardly surprising to find Rommel, like other German officers, an enthusiastic reader of Liddell Hart when his books began appearing in German in the 1920s and 1930s.

Of all Rommel's actions in World War I, undoubtedly his greatest triumph was his participation in the capture of Mount Mataiur. The Austrians, fighting both the Russians and, after May 1915, the Italians, had found themselves constantly facing crises from which they required extrication by their German allies. In the autumn of 1917 it was Italy which was posing the greater threat and after 10 battles along the banks of the Isonzo, their Commander in Chief, General Cadorna, launched an eleventh and then a twelfth attack with Trieste as his objective. As the struggle developed, the Austrians began to realize their own inability to hold out. Seven veteran German divisions were accordingly welded into a new Fourteenth Army with Rommel's mountain troops attached to it. In early October, therefore, he found himself in Carinthia, his losses in Rumania having been made good.

The battlefield was a mountainous region with the enemy well-ensconced in positions along the peaks and ridges. These overlooked the Austro-German lines in the valley of the Isonzo and, according to Rommel, the Italians were

well supplied with both artillery and ammunition which they used in constant and remorseless interdiction fire. This, however, was likely to be the least of the attackers' troubles since in the offensive proper they would have to scale the inhospitable heights to get to grips with the enemy.

Rommel's unit was assigned to the center of the line opposite Mount Mataiur, part of the Kolovrat range. The capture of Mataiur had been entrusted to the Bavarian Infantry Life Guards with the mountaineers following in the support wave. However Rommel, finding this secondary role little to his taste, managed to persuade his commander to allow him to move his axis a little to the right so that he could attack the Italian positions independently.

What followed bore once again the plain marks of Rommel's style. Leading his troops up the steep defiles, taking advantage of the predawn darkness and such cover as the terrain offered, his detachment infiltrated the Italian lines. At first light they overran an Italian artillery position, taking the gun crews with the bayonet and without a shot having been fired. Leaving one company to hold open the gap they had formed and, if possible, widen it, he pushed on with the other. He was forced to return, however, when the first group was attacked by an entire Italian battalion. Taken in the rear they quickly gave in and he sent back 4000 prisoners and, with them, the message that the line was breached. His commander, reinforcing success, sent him four more companies and with these he began penetrating the line in depth. He managed to get his forces across the main road leading to Mount Mataiur where, among other achievements, he captured 2000 men of the crack 4th Bersaglieri Brigade.

Even this was not enough. He decided to go for Mataiur itself by an advance straight across country. At dawn the following day he himself with two other officers and a handful of men walked straight into the camp of another Italian elite unit, the Salerno Brigade, and demanded their surrender which was offered after brief hesitation.

This is a necessarily brief description of what was in fact a highly complex action. It lasted in all 50 hours, during the whole of which his detachment were either fighting or on the move. They had repeatedly scaled heights of thousands of feet with some of the men carrying heavy machine guns and other weapons. The German Alpine Corps order of the day for 3 November recognized this achievement. The capture of the Kolov-rat Range had, it said, caused the collapse of the whole enemy defensive structure and it singled out the capture of Mataiur as pivotal. The Rommel detachment had taken as prisoner 150 officers and 9000 men, besides 81 guns and other booty. Its own losses amounted to six dead and 30 wounded.

Personal recognition came in the form of his own promotion to captain. All that now remained to bring the offensive to its conclusion was the pursuit of the enemy. They were by no means routed, however, and stood and resisted wherever the opportunity to do so presented itself

as, in this region of mountain and river valley, it often did, so that Rommel and his men were constantly in action. On one occasion, he and a few bold spirits waded the fast-flowing and icy cold River Piave to lead the way for a surprise attack on the village of Longarone. In the ensuing action not only was the village captured, but a number of prisoners, taken earlier by the Italians, were liberated.

The struggle lasted through the last week of October and into November, but it was more or less over by the 10th and in trophies of war Rommel's unit had done even better than at Mataiur, their booty including 18 mountain cannons, two semiautomatic cannon, over 600 pack animals, 250 loaded vehicles, 10 trucks and two ambulances. In addition there were 10,000 prisoners. His own losses were six dead and 22 wounded or missing.

Some fighting remained and this continued until the turn of the year with the Württemberg Mountain Battalion acquiring further honors. Its last action under Rommel's command took place late on the night 1 January 1918 when its positions at Pallone and on Mount Tomba were attacked by an Italian raiding party. A jammed heavy machine gun handicapped the defenders and its two-man crew died trying to get it back into action. The attackers were beaten off, just the same.

Thereafter Rommel was sent back to Germany on leave and 'to his great sorrow' was not to return to his Württembergers. Instead he was given a staff posting which he occupied until the end of the war.

It is true that his successes had not always received the notice they deserved from his superiors and that they had also bred jealousies among his fellow officers. He was very well aware of this, as he was very conscious – perhaps overconscious – of his own capabilities.

One has, of course, to set him against the backdrop of the German army of his day. Able, superbly organized, the German General Staff was, all the same, dominated by an arrogant and autocratic aristocracy. We know, for example, that when in August 1914 Moltke decided on Erich Ludendorff as commander of the Eighth Army in East Prussia, he was compelled also to find a man with the requisite 'von' to share command.

Rommel came from a lower middle-class milieu. He was serving in a modest, line regiment. He realized this put him at a disadvantage and felt it as a gross

Above: General Ludendorff was in effective command of the German Armies in France in 1918.

injustice. From numerous recorded comments it is obvious he had little time for the run of General Staff officers. 'Men of marble,' he called them, 'with cold, black hearts.' If he admired Napoleon more than any German soldier, it is certain that among other reasons it was because he had made the French army into the 'carrière ouverte aux talents,' a change which had yet to reach Germany. In these circumstances, one can well understand the delight he felt when he succeeded in taking Mount Mataiur in advance of the Life Guards.

Yet that entire action can only have reinforced his feelings of being displaced by his social superiors. There is a curious custom in the German army whereby decorations are promised in advance for the successful completion of a particular task. This happened in the case of the struggle for the Kolovrat Range. Rommel quite rightly felt that he and his mountaineers had achieved the first significant victory by their breaking of the enemy front. Yet the promised *Pour le Mérite* was given to Ferdinand Schörner commanding the Bavarians.

There was worse to come; in the storming of Mount Mataiur victory was ascribed not to Rommel, but to a Lieutenant Walther Schnieber. He too was awarded a *Pour le Mérite*. Rommel, doubly incensed, went so far as to persuade the German Official Historians after the war to amend their account of the engagement so that he received proper credit. The *Pour le Mérite* which we know he was aching for was not awarded to him until after the taking of Longarone.

Left: Discarded Italian equipment litters the roadside as a supply column passes by to the front during the Isonzo fighting.

2: THE PEACETIME WARRIOR

The immediate postwar period is remembered by most Germans as a gray passage of misery. If the enormous casualty lists had ceased to appear, so too had the accounts of victories and heroism which had enlivened those days. In the cold streets, as autumn gave way to winter, the wounded hobbled and begged, the lines of unemployed ex-soldiers shuffled disconsolately toward the doors of the relief agencies and soup kitchens tried to minister to the hungry. Sometimes an old man or woman or a child collapsed on the cobbles from hunger or cold. No one appeared much moved by the sight. Occasionally violence would erupt between political factions or the Communist or Socialist parties would mount one of those mass demonstrations of grim-faced, cheerless working men which had so deeply impressed the young Hitler, himself soon to join the ex-service unemployed.

The country seemed to be suffering every form of national adversity. A long and bloody war had ended in defeat. Existing economic problems were exacerbated by a punitive and extortionate peace forced upon it without opportunity for negotiation in 1919. In 1918 units of the Imperial Navy at Kiel had mutinied. Communism had inspired this rising, and fanned by economic distress, discontent spread especially in 'Red Berlin.' The right blamed an unnatural alliance of the subversives in Germany and the rapacity of Germany's erstwhile enemies – Britain, France and the United States for the troubles. The armies had never been defeated, they claimed. They had been betrayed by the first and tricked by the second. Even General Erich Ludendorff, the former commander in chief who, by his loss of nerve was the man most directly responsible for the call for an armistice, soon saw events in this more flattering light.

While the right recognized that the effects of Allied chicanery could not be countered immediately, they were impatient to come to grips with the internal traitors. The result was the recruitment of Freikorps units all over the country, their membership composed mainly of officers unemployed now the army had been reduced to less than a tenth of its former size under the terms of the 'dictated' Versailles peace treaty. They instituted a reign of political murder and terror against which the government, as

Right: Mutinous soldiers in Berlin in November 1918. They are supporters of the left-wing Soldiers Council.
Below: French and American troops parade in Koblenz in 1919 during the Allied occupation.

it repeatedly told the protesting Allies, was impotent.

There was, of course, some truth in this excuse. Nonetheless, there were also those, at least in the bureaucracy of the tiny army, who saw certain advantages in having trained men available in the Freikorps. Incontrovertible evidence exists to prove the link between them and the army. Some of its groups went so far as to pursue an overtly double life. For a few weeks they would be numbered as part of a Reichswehr unit. Then perhaps because some Allied truce commissioner began asking awkward questions, they would slip out of barracks to pursue an independent career and re-return when the hue and cry was over. As the Freikorps were often dealing with militarism's avowed enemies – the pacifists, Socialists and Communists – there is little doubt that the army was providing at least part of its funding.

What was Rommel's position in all this? Peace, and especially such a peace as his country was experiencing, could only have been an agony to him. He was the complete soldier, the man of action whose memory harked back to the triumphs of Mount Mataiur and Longarone. If a peacetime Rommel is hard to picture, a civilian one is unthinkable and, had he been forced to become one, he might well have turned toward the Freikorps, though innate conservatism, the esteem for authority of the 'eldest son' would have caused him some conflict. Fortunately, the question did not arise. His transfer to the staff late in the war had had one useful consequence: he got to know the right people and unlike many of his comrades was able to stay in the army. On the other hand, it would be absurd to suppose he knew nothing of the Freikorps or their conduct and his disapproval seems at least to have been muted.

However, his immediate horizons in the weeks after the Armistice stretched no further than his wife, Lucie, who was ill in Danzig. He intended to bring her back to his mother's home in Weingarten, Danzig itself having been created a 'Free City,' though actually largely under Polish control, by the Versailles Treaty. In the turmoil of Germany at

Above: Captain Basil Liddell Hart influenced young German officers like Rommel and Guderian.

that time such a journey was a hazardous undertaking for an officer in uniform. He made it just the same and seems to have suffered nothing more than an occasional insult from rebellious elements and, once, narrowly missed arrest.

In March 1919 with Lucie now recovered, he was sent to Friedrichshafen to command 'No 32 Internal Security Company.' This turned out to be a body of German sailors with marked Communist leanings and in no mood to accept command. Rommel seems to have brought them to heel, for they were soon being used against other disaffected bodies. In the spring of 1920, for instance, they held back an angry mob trying to force its way into the town hall at Gmund. In a tactic later to become almost habitual among European 'security forces,' he turned fire hoses on the crowd.

The political squabblings of the right and left were to persist, especially in the larger towns for the rest of the decade. However by the middle of 1920 the Weimar Government felt sufficiently confident that the danger of a successful Communist putsch had been averted, to relax its guard a little. In the October of that year Rommel was transferred to a rifle company, part of an infantry regiment, based in Stuttgart. Here he remained for the next nine years.

Ambitious German soldiers were beginning to study the works of writers like Liddell Hart and General J F C Fuller. Their thesis seemed to have a particular relevance to the post-Versailles German forces. Liddell Hart turned on its head the trend of recent wars toward ever bigger weapons. They had become dinosaurs, he asserted, so huge they could scarcely move and so tied down the whole struggle. His own tactical ideas

Left: Supporters of the right-wing Kapp Putsch in Berlin in 1920. Note the Swastika emblem on the side of the truck.

depended on light, nimble, but hard-hitting forces used in strong concentrations. Once having pierced the enemy line, these would pour through the breach they had made for themselves, penetrating far into the rear.

This is exactly what German soldiers, sailors and airmen wanted to hear. Instead of the Treaty of Versailles condemning them and their country to permanent weakness for lack of the big battalions of their enemies, it would, on the contrary, allow them to build up resources of the mobile weapons permitted to them and it was these, a great expert was telling them, which would command tomorrow's conflicts.

Among those who read, marked and inwardly digested all this had been one of the country's outstanding military minds. General Hans von Seeckt had been the architect of one of the old Germany's most resplendent victories in the recent war – the breakthrough of the Russian lines in Eastern Poland in the spring of 1915. The train of seemingly

endless Austro-German victories which followed not only brought their forces within striking distance of the Russian capital, Petrograd (now Leningrad) and to the edges of the grain belt of the Ukraine, it also broke the resistance of the Czarist military machine which finally crumbled in revolution two years later.

Despite his traditional background, von Seeckt recognized that the application of new principles called for an army which was unfettered by an outdated philosophy. Social class must cease to be the principal determinant of promotion. Merit alone should decide preferment. This would also mean severing the traditional link between the army and the political right which, in any case, made it suspect among the republican and social democrat politicians who ruled postwar Germany. The army would be apolitical with the role of upholding the constitution whatever government happened to be in power. Seeckt showed himself as good as his word when he

threatened to use his troops to suppress the Nazi-inspired Bürgerbräukeller putsch of November 1923, notwithstanding the fact that one of the country's most famous soldiers, Erich Ludendorff, was playing a leading role in it. (Seeckt was never to see the final realization of his plans as soon after becoming president of the republic, a jealous Hindenburg dismissed him.)

All in all, it can be confidently stated that Rommel would have found the new German army – for all the constraints and limitations an unjust peace treaty imposed – far more congenial than the one he had joined in 1910. He was not an aristocrat, had indeed suffered at their hands as in the affair of his *Pour le Mérite*. He was, besides, a natural democrat by temperament with the ability to mix with all sorts and conditions of men.

In any case, the tactics now being propounded were precisely those he had

Below: A Nazi artist's impression of an early meeting of the party. Hitler joined the party in late 1919.

used with such success – though with the difference that he had had to rely on the legs and energies of his infantrymen to carry them through enemy lines, where in future they would be borne through them in tanks, armored cars and tracked personnel vehicles.

He filled his spare moments by studying the internal-combustion engine and came to know more about it than many mechanics, as some were to find to their chagrin. He showed a similar interest in weaponry, especially the machine gun, dismantling, studying, reassembling any he could lay hands on. It was, one could say, an ideal apprenticeship for the man who was one day so to distinguish himself as an armor commander.

He was also devoting time to sport and physical recreation not only for himself, but for his men. There are ample indications that they did not always take kindly to it, especially to early morning physical jerks. Their protests were usually unavailing.

As to other activities, he showed an entrenched bourgeois philistinism. When he was not pulling motorcycles or machine guns apart, he was attending to his stamp collection or out walking his dog. He was not even particular about his food, drank little and his only sortie in the fine arts was to take up the violin which he had learned in boyhood. Music failed, however, to captivate him. In one letter to Lucie he refers to a visit to the ballet, which bored him. Once, in Italy during World War II, he was guest at a gala performance at the Milan Opera House. In an interval when all about him were in raptures about the music and singing, he was holding an impromptu staff conference to discuss a plan he had formulated during the performance. His aides attest that philosophy or culture were rare subjects of conversation in his presence. Never in any of his letters home does he hint that he had been impressed by anything seen in either architecture or landscape. What to others was a beauty spot, he seems to have appraised solely in terms of military potential. When he took his men into the

Above right: Men of the SA pictured in Neustadt during the abortive Nazi putsch in 1923.
Right: The Karl Liebknechthaus, the Berlin HQ of the German Communists. Rommel and the army tried to keep out of Nazi-Communist battles.

Above: Frau Goebbels after voting in 1933. The Nazis became the largest single party after the elections of March 1933 but never had a majority in any free elections.

countryside it was to teach them to improvise bivouacs or rafts for river crossings.

Such attitudes were quite consistent with German High Command traditions and probably impressed his superiors. (Once when Alfried von Schlieffen, Chief of the General Staff between 1891 and 1906, and formulator of the plan for the attack on France of 1914, was out on a morning ride, a young aide pointed out the glory of the sun sparkling on the River Pregel, the general glared at it for a moment, then commented, 'An unimportant obstacle.')

Thus from all points of view Rommel was admirable military material. He might have driven his men hard, but he also cared for their welfare, recognizing that they were more than fighting automata. He organized dances and other distractions to help make their off-duty hours tolerable and there is little doubt

he was personally liked and admired.

In 1929 his skill in handling men was given formal recognition when he was appointed an instructor at the Infantry School at Dresden. In October he moved to that city, taking with him not only Lucie, but his one-year-old son, Manfred, born the previous Christmas Eve.

Like his British and French counterparts, his war experience had engendered a horror of the wanton expenditure of human life and a determination not to be party to its repetition. As was the case with his desert adversary, Montgomery, he was never so pleased as when he could secure a victory – as he had often done in the Italian campaign – with the minimum of loss of life by either his own men or among the enemy. He would certainly have seconded the proposition of another desert foe, Field Marshal Sir Archibald Wavell, that 'a big butcher's bill is no proof of sound strategy.' In fact, he believed that a commander's skill was measured in lives saved rather than in lives squandered. As a consequence of this, the first principle he tried to incul-

cate into the future officers entrusted to his charge at Dresden was 'how to save lives.'

As a lecturer he was extremely popular with a repertoire which included descriptions and analyses of the actions he had seen in France and Italy. He recognized the value of what are now called 'visual aids,' projecting sketch maps and drawings to illustrate his points. The climax of the series was always the assault on Mount Mataiur, and some who heard him during his four years at the Infantry School and recalled him as they knew him later felt that this had been the high point of his entire military life beside which even the desert victories paled.

Rommel's superiors and peers who were to become quite scant in their praise of him were less stinting at this time. He was 'a sterling character,' had 'great military gifts,' was 'an exemplary commander,' 'a towering personality even among hand-picked officers,' 'a genuine leader type, inspiring cheerful confidence in others,' 'first rate infantry and combat instructor,' 'respected by his colleagues, worshipped by his cadets.'

What could be said of him then, could equally well have been said throughout his career, though, in fairness, it must be observed that similar praise was accorded to other young German officers, not all of whom rose to his high rank.

The early months of 1933 had seen the triumph of the National Socialist Party and the accession of Hitler to the Chancellorship, both having been consistently and decisively rejected by the German electorate previously. Rommel is on record as declaring the Nazis to have been 'a bunch of scallywags.' Such a view would have been consistent with a temperament which rejected radicalism whether from left or right.

At the same time, he undoubtedly welcomed the promise of resurgent German militarism which formed one of the main planks of the National Socialist platform. Certainly, from his later statements and conduct, it is plain he did not include Hitler in his denunciation and one can only suppose he did not allow his feelings about the party go further than comparatively innocuous verbal form. The epithet 'scallywags' would have been one which many Nazis would have found more complimentary than otherwise. Had he been more forceful in condemnation or more active in obstruction, it would scarcely have escaped notice or reprisal.

In fact, he continued to progress in his chosen profession. In October 1933, promoted to major, he was given command of the 3rd Battalion, 17th Infantry Regiment, a rifle unit, and posted to Goslar in the Harz mountains. He at once impressed his new brothers-in-arms by passing an initiative test of climbing then skiing down one of the local slopes. Having done so once, he then suggested a repetition and then yet another. When he proposed a fourth attempt, however, he could find no one willing to accompany him. Priding themselves on toughness, they were forced to concede that they had met their match. When he reverted to his favorite pursuits of riding, hunting and shooting among the neighboring forests, he insisted that they

Above right: Field Marshal von Hindenburg was president of Germany from 1925–34. He did not like the Nazis but was more worried about Communism. **Right:** Hitler addresses the Reichstag. Goering, the Speaker, sits behind.

Above: Propaganda Minister Goebbels addresses a Nazi meeting in 1934.
Left: Rommel's first meeting with Hitler. Hitler inspects the guard of honor. Major Rommel, with Iron Cross, is to the left.

should do the same, presumably on the theory that stalking four-footed prey would serve in stalking the two-footed variety of a future war, a war he, like many others, thought inevitable.

The cult of hardiness was one which Rommel sought to extend to his family. The long-suffering Lucie was dragged up mountains in an effort to make her learn to ski, or compelled to plunge into the waters of lake or sea to learn swimming. At the age of seven, his son Manfred was taken off to a stable to be taught to ride, an enterprise which had to be kept secret from his mother. However Rommel the husband and father overlooked the basic fact that they were not among those bound to subservience to him and frequently lost the struggles of will. Taken to a mountain top, Lucie simply refused to ski down and had to be allowed to take the lift. Sent to the topmost diving board at a swimming pool at the age of eight and directed to jump into the water so far below, Manfred, with his father's cadets watching gleefully, refused on the ground that as his

father was wearing riding boots he would be unable to dive to his rescue if the need arose.

It is all too easy to see this preoccupation with physical fitness from the standpoint of our own times and condemn it as no more than a manifestation of the military mind. This is not so. The age was one in which throughout Europe and to a great extent America, a fetish was made of 'keeping fit.' This extended to the most emancipated and liberal of the age, those who today would rush on to the streets in protest if they felt their children were being subjected to this kind of thing.

It was while at Goslar that Rommel met Hitler for the first time. Though there is some debate about the exact date, it was probably in 1934 when the Führer went to that town to meet a farmers' delegation and to participate in a kind of secular Harvest Festival. The vagueness surrounding the date is curious, for not only did Rommel come under Hitler's sway from this time, but there is little doubt, as time progressed, that the German leader provided the father-figure he had unconsciously sought.

Enthusiasm for Hitler is not altogether incomprehensible. Like many of his fellow countrymen, Rommel felt that

in the months after Hitler's assumption of power there were all the signs that a new era was dawning. The unemployed were disappearing from the streets, the economy was being stabilized and, even more important, there was a feeling of returning national pride and confidence among the people at large.

Nor was this enthusiasm limited to Germany – at least at first. Abroad there was the feeling that Germany had suffered enough and in the interests not only of itself but of Europe as a whole, needed a period of stability and prosperity. In France where there was in many quarters fear of the Front Populaire of Communists and Socialists acceding to power, Hitler was seen as a welcome and strategically placed bulwark against the Soviet Union. Nor could the Conservatives in Britain and the United States look other than with relief at the shift rightward his advent represented. The left wing of the British Labour Party were totally deceived by the word 'Socialist' in the title of his party and by Goebbels's adroit presentation of it as a working-class movement.

Despite all this, the attempt to present Rommel as just another political innocent whose only interest in Hitler or his party arose from patriotism and a desire to advance the cause of the army, where

Above: This picture was taken in April 1934. The persecution of the Jews was extended by the Nuremberg Decrees, issued in March 1935.

intuition but sheer idiocy. Not even his most sycophantic apologists have been able to evade the conclusion, fully demonstrated by later behavior, that Rommel was a racist who, for example, thought it desperately unfair that the British should employ 'black' – by which he meant Indian – troops against a white adversary.

There is no room for doubt that Rommel was convinced of the merits of National Socialism. He signed postcards to intimate friends, 'Heil Hitler,' a practice which though encouraged by the party, was derisively resisted by most Germans. He repeated and approved Hitler's assertions that the army should be an instrument of the nation's political will, which was a long way from von Seeckt's policy. After meeting some Swiss army officers, he reported delightedly not only that they had expressed sympathy with the aspirations of the New Germany, but also that they had spoken with 'remarkable understanding of our Jewish problem.'

The year 1934 had seen the removal of the one doubt the army still retained about the new government. The National Socialist Party had built up a private army during its 'time of struggle,' the SA (for *Sturm Abteilung* or Storm Detachments). Although there were instances of collusion between the SA and regular forces, as an institution the army more often found itself in conflict with the Nazis who saw the constitution Seeckt had set it to protect as the product of the 'November Traitors.' Furthermore the leader of the SA, Ernst Röhm, himself an ex-soldier, had frequently declared that his forces were to form the nucleus of a new German army with himself as commander in chief.

If this should happen, soldiers like Rommel, who were not party members – Seeckt had prohibited all political activity, even voting – could well find themselves elbowed out. Luckily for them, Hitler had misgivings of his own. Röhm was too arrogant and the conduct of his men often an embarrassment at home and abroad. But the SA leader also made it plain he regarded himself and his Praetorian Guard as the chief instrument of Hitler's accession to power. It was, therefore, all too obvious that the Caesar they had made they could also unmake if he failed to please them.

Like all those leaders who are the

after all he earned his bread and butter, must fail on one ground. In 1923 Hitler had written *Mein Kampf*. Among the plethora of rancid diatribes those against the Jews predominate. They include the declaration that had 12,000–15,000 of 'these Hebrew enemies' been gassed at the beginning of World War I, 'the sacrifice of millions at the front would not have been in vain.'

If, as is likely, Rommel never read *Mein Kampf*, the message can still hardly

have escaped him, for it was Hitler's most constant theme. When he attacked the Versailles Diktat and promised to renounce it, which was what every German and not least those in uniform wanted to hear, he did so only because he regarded it as part of the worldwide Jewish conspiracy. When he examined any of the questions of the day from the League of Nations to the 'degeneracy of modern art,' it was always to conclude they were symptoms of the same plot, exhibited equally in bourgeois capitalism and Bolshevik Communism.

To have missed this would have required of Rommel not lack of political product of revolution, Hitler recognized that his position would be secure only if he destroyed the revolution makers. In the 'Night of the Long Knives' in June 1934 kangaroo courts were established under the aegis of the SS, a body whose loyalty to Hitler was beyond question, and in suddenness and terrible secrecy Röhm and scores of his paladins were arraigned, sentenced and executed. In this way the position, not only of Germany's leaders, but also of its army was made secure. The relief in military circles was tangible, even if Rommel privately expressed disapproval of the methods employed. If they expected to enjoy an independent existence, the soldiers were soon to be disappointed. With the death of the president von Hindenburg in 1935, his office was fused with that of chancellor under the new title of 'Führer.' With it went command in chief of the armed forces. Hitler was shrewd enough to make the oath of allegiance not one to the office, but to himself personally. Like it or not, the army had become his own instrument.

Whatever his own feelings about the

SA may have been, Rommel was to be brought into intimate contact with it. Far from forming its framework, the rump of the SA left over from the Röhm purge was actually absorbed into the army. In 1935 Rommel was given the task of trying to turn these men into soldiers. Often the least employable of the unemployed – many of them were former Communists who had defected when their own party seemed to lack a future – they were little more than a collection of street-corner rowdies and bar-room bullies for whom the SA gave unbridled opportunity for violence. With belligerence as their sole military virtue they defied even Rommel's attempts to refashion them and the experiment was soon abandoned.

Hitler, meanwhile, had been as good as his word over the renunciation of the Treaty of Versailles. The German army was, therefore, in the throes of expansion. This, of necessity, meant its regular officers became, as had long been intended, the training cadres. Rommel, now a lieutenant colonel and having passed the staff examinations which

made him one of his nation's military elect, was posted to the Potsdam War Academy in October 1935 and was once more an instructor.

Even at Potsdam he was not to escape the tentacles of the party, for he was asked as a special assignment to help improve Hitler Youth discipline. This was certainly a more congenial experience than his previous one with the SA. He liked young people and had the knack of getting on with them, largely because he treated them as equals, which was obviously extremely flattering considering he was, to them, a most distinguished soldier.

Nevertheless, a rift developed between him and the leader of the movement, Baldur von Schirach. Schirach felt his movement was being given too military a cast and objected when it was proposed to draft unmarried Wehrmacht officers as instructors. There is little doubt Rommel saw it as what it ultimately be-

Below: With Hitler are a local Nazi leader, Röhm of the SA and Himmler of the SS. The army leaders were pleased at Röhm's downfall.

came, a kindergarten for the army, where young Germans began the process of indoctrination which turned them into young fanatics whose greatest ambition was to die for the Führer.

In fact it is plain, whatever the merits of their cases, that Rommel and von Schirach were two men who rubbed one another up the wrong way, so that the ever touchy lieutenant colonel was perpetually seeing slights, perhaps because Schirach came from the aristocracy. When at a gala performance at a theater the Hitler Youth Leader was given a seat in the front row and the other relegated to one behind him, Rommel ostentatiously moved into a vacant seat in the front with the remark that their's was a state in which 'the Wehrmacht came first.'

Although no effort was spared to involve him, Hitler always stood aloof from the ceaseless quarrels which went on round him. He preferred to put personal animosities to his own use on the principle of 'divide and rule.' Accordingly, the quarrel between an army officer and the Hitler Youth leader affected the career of neither man.

Actually Rommel's next contact with his Führer was more or less fortuitous. In September 1936 Rommel was put in charge of security arrangements at the year's Party Rally at Nuremberg – the most amibitious yet held. When Hitler decided he wanted to escape the official round by driving into the country, Rommel was given orders to ensure the minimum of party functionaries accompanied him. The leader's car left, the first three succeeding cars were allowed to go, but all subsequent ones halted, despite the fulminations of their passengers, often men of high rank. To prevent their catching up by using side roads, a system of army road blocks was set up. Afterward Hitler thanked Rommel personally.

The following year the German leader's attention was again drawn to Rommel. His book *Infantry Attacks* had been published early in that year and quickly became something of a best seller. Indeed royalties from it were soon to cause its author a tax problem and he had to make special arrangements to

Left: Hitler with young members of the Hitler Youth. Rommel quarrelled with von Schirach, the Hitler Youth leader.

Left: Baldur von Schirach joins Hitler in greeting a crowd of Nazi supporters. Schirach was later Gauleiter of Vienna.

annexed and shortly after his return from the Sudetenland, Rommel, now a full colonel, was posted as commander of the War Academy at Wiener Neustadt outside Vienna. He arrived on 10 November, a day infamous in German history as the 'Kristallnacht,' the night when Nazi mobs burned and looted Jewish shops, homes and synagogues as a reprisal for the murder of a minor German diplomatic official in Paris. With wife and son, he moved into a bungalow near the academy and set to work to make it the most up-to-date center of military instruction in the Greater Reich.

In his first year there were two brief interruptions of the achievement of this ambition. He was given command of Hitler's mobile headquarters for the occupation of Prague. The Führer's

protect his growing fortune. It was duly read by Hitler and admired.

Was it the book or his recollection of Rommel's cunning at the Nuremberg Rally which led to his appointment as commander of the military escort which was to accompany Hitler on a tour of the newly ceded Sudeten territories of Czechoslovakia? Probably neither. Other German soldiers had produced works Hitler had admired. Notable among them was Hans Guderian whose *Achtung – Panzer!* provided the ground plan for using massed armor as an instrument of assault. Gratitude for such service was never a very lively or enduring sentiment in the Führer's make up – he simply expected that everyone around him should serve him with maximum energy and efficiency – and it is unlikely that he felt any permanent obligation over the Nuremberg incident. In any event, through the appointment Rommel found himself on equal terms with some of the Nazi leadership. A picture taken by Hoffman, Hitler's personal photographer, shows him seated at a table on the Führer's train with Himmler, the SS chief, at his side and both roaring with laughter.

In the spring of 1938 Austria had been

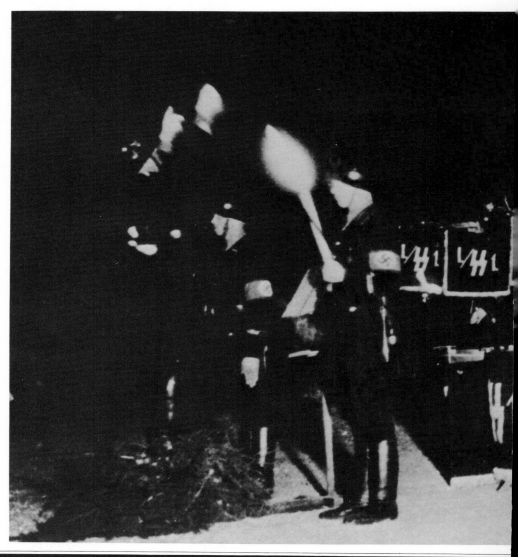

Right: Ceremonial displays like this were used by Goebbel's Propaganda Ministry to reinforce the message of German strength.

Right: Mussolini, Hitler, a German
official and Chamberlain at Munich in
September 1938 during the Sudeten crisis.

personal SS guard, the *Leibstandarte
Adolf Hitler* failed to turn up at the
border rendezvous point because of a
blizzard. Rommel, nonetheless, persuaded him he must drive into the city
and undertook to protect him virtually
single-handed. 'I made him come with
me,' he said later, and claimed that this
advice was never forgotten. Only eight
days later, he accompanied Hitler when
he sailed into Memel 'voluntarily' returned to Germany by Lithuania.

Rommel, like too many Germans of
the time, saw all these adventures, which
the world viewed as naked aggression
against weak neighbors, as further proof
that the nation's confidence and dynamism was reasserting itself. If faced
with criticism of such policies, he would
no doubt have answered, as others did,

Above: Although athletes like Jesse Owens disproved the claims of Aryan supremacy at the 1936 Olympics German propaganda ignored this.

that his country was simply doing what other European nations and notably Britain had done, acquiring territory – *Lebensraum* or living space as it was then called. He was delighted when the pessimistic fears of the General Staff, who from the time of the reoccupation of the Rhineland, had constantly forecast an angry reaction from France and Britain, were shown to have been wrong.

In 1939 he was optimistic enough to believe that Hitler's latest *démarche* – that against Poland to secure Danzig and its corridor for Germany – would be successful. However, if Hitler's unique and, up to now, successful combination of bluff and intimidation failed to work, then like most army officers, Rommel was prepared to contemplate war with something akin to excitement. Internationally, the Poles were regarded as no insignificant military power. Though their army was smaller than Germany's, it was known to be in a high state of readiness and had defeated the Russians in 1919–20. It was likely, therefore, to prove a real test of German mettle.

There was a corresponding belief that the German armed forces were ready for battle, vastly enlarged since Hitler's accession to power six years earlier. Training and equipment had both been adapted to suit the needs of the German armed forces' revolutionary strategy, which the world was soon to call by the German name *Blitzkrieg*, and which was basically the first practical application of

Liddell Hart's 'expanding torrent.' Tried out on the hapless Spaniards during their Civil War, it had shown its immense potential. The lessons learned on the Iberian proving ground had been applied and there was an almost desperate anxiety to put them to use.

Europe had sat apprehensively by, limiting opposition to diplomatic criticism, but observing with alarm, the growing strength which Germany flaunted quite openly not only at the annual Nuremberg Rallies, but in 1936 at the Berlin Olympic Games, an occasion supposedly devoted to the cause of peace.

A threat to Poland had led the West and especially France and Britain to renew their disapproving noises, but no one in Germany seriously believed it would come to anything and in any case how were two countries with the landmass of Germany itself separating them from Poland to offer their ally any tangible help? A speedy victory on the Polish plains would face them with a *fait accompli* and force them to come to terms with reality. As to the rights and wrongs of the matter, reading only the

Above: The Luftwaffe was employed to support Franco during the Spanish Civil War. General Sperrle gives orders at Santander airfield.

German newspapers (Rommel himself was a devotee of the party's *Völkischer Beobachter*) and hearing only the broadcasts of Goebbels's *Reichs Rundfunk*, they saw only Polish intransigence over an issue which affected vital German interests. Danzig was a German city with a predominantly German population.

3: POLAND AND FRANCE

Hitler intended to launch his invasion of Poland on 26 August although it was postponed until 1 September. Among the numerous visitors to the Reich Chancellery in the preceding days was Rommel, now 47, who was told he had been promoted to major general. He was plainly ecstatic and wrote to his wife to tell her how he left the building 'as a brand-new general, in a brand-new general's uniform.'

The appointment which followed was something of an anticlimax all the same. He would have liked an active command, instead he was cast in the role with which he had already become familiar, that of guarding his Führer as headquarters commandant. This time there is no doubt that he was the personal choice of Hitler who had taken a liking to the down-to-earth soldier from Württemberg, perhaps because, as Desmond Young suggests, he was not one of those titled officers with whom Hitler was always ill at ease suspecting that they secretly despised his own origins. One mark of favor was that Rommel's promotion was backdated to 1 June.

In the event, his appointment brought him closer to the fighting in Poland and allowed him to observe it more closely and for longer than he had expected.

Hitler arrived at his advanced headquarters in Pomerania on the Polish border on 4 September for what everyone, including his headquarters commandant expected was to be a brief visit of duty to the front. As it was, he was unable to tear himself away and stayed throughout the campaign, advancing his headquarters as the front line itself advanced, even insisting on going further forward than his security advisers thought prudent, into areas still not entirely subdued.

Rommel was once more mixing with the upper echelons of the party and while he despised some of them, men like the crude and brutal Martin Bormann, he was delighted to report to Lucie and Manfred that he had dined at the Führer's table.

Though always fascinated by new weapons of war, Rommel was primarily an infantry officer. What he saw in Poland, however, seems to have fired him with new ambitions. The great and

Right: Hitler watches German troops crossing the River San during the Polish campaign.
Below: Observing the fighting in Poland. Rommel is immediately to the right of Hitler. Others present include Keitel and von Reichenau.

glorious victories of the future would, he realized, be won, not by the men on foot, but by the men in tanks and he desperately wanted to be among them. After the fall of Poland, Hitler was in a generous mood. What, he asked Rommel, did he most desire? Without hesitation he answered, 'Command of a Panzer division' and as though from a fairy godfather his request was granted.

The end of the Polish campaign was followed by a period of uncertainty for there was a feeling that the war might now end. In aid of their ally, the British and French had made only the feeblest of token gestures. On the German side there was reason to hope, therefore, as Rommel put it in a letter to Lucie, that the war might 'peter out.' By their declaration on Poland's behalf, the Allies had done their bounden duty. That country had fallen, nonetheless. What point was there in continuing the quarrel? If suitable terms could be arranged, peace might be managed. Hitler made a bid for it in a speech in the Reichstag in early October, tendering the olive branch with his left hand while keeping the right bunched into a menacing fist. Pusillanimous the Anglo-French leadership might be, but even they could not swallow this.

The question which faced OKH (*Oberkommando des Heeres* or Army High Command) was: how soon could the German forces be brought back from the east and redirected west? November, urged Hitler. This was impractical because, for one thing, the Polish campaign had demonstrated certain deficiencies in the military machine which needed correction before it could be thrown against the more formidable western enemy. Nothing could be done before the New Year. Then the German plans, quite literally, miscarried. On 10 January an officer bearing them force-landed his aircraft in Belgium and was captured before he could destroy his briefcase.

It was a blessing in disguise for the German strategy and for Rommel personally. The captured plans represented a nadir in German General Staff thinking. They had already been severely criticized in many quarters and one general had gone so far in condemning them as to pronounce them like 'British General Staff plans.' They were, in fact, little more than a recasting of the von Schlieffen Plan of 1914 with its mass advance through Belgium before the armies swung west to cross the French frontier. That Germany had actually lost the war which it embarked on with these plans seems not to have worried anyone too greatly. The truth was that the General Staff did not expect either this plan or any other to succeed against the Anglo-French forces and regarded its preparation as little more than an academic exercise.

However, since they were now public knowledge among the enemy, there was no alternative to redrafting. What finally emerged was due mainly to Erich von Manstein, a critic of the earlier plan. It was so great an improvement that Hitler was quick to claim it as his own brainchild.

The main French strength was mustered along the Maginot Line, a string of interlocking fortresses connected with each other by an elaborate system of

underground tunnels and railroads. This ran almost the length of the Franco-German border, but tailed off abruptly in the northeast, in the area round Longwy. Here was an area of forest which the French General Staff had convinced themselves was impassable, though von Clausewitz had once called it 'the stomach of France.'

The Maginot Line forces were to be engaged by Army Group C, under Field Marshal Wilhelm Ritter von Leeb. A second force, Army Group B, would, meanwhile, advance into Belgium and Holland – the latter being something of an afterthought by Hitler who considered the Dutch ports might serve in a later invasion of Britain. With luck, the Anglo-French forces would unseat themselves from their well-prepared positions along the Belgian frontier to race to the aid of the two invaded neutrals. Not only would this catch them off balance, it would also leave the way clear for the third and crucial stage of the assault, a rapid advance by armored units out of the 'impassable' Forest of Ardennes and right down to the French coast. The defenders, those in the Low countries and those in France, would thus be effectively cut off from one another. The extremely appropriate code name applied to this was *Unternehmung Sichelschnitt* (Operation Scythe-Stroke).

Reformulation of plans had taken time, but this at least meant that Rommel was able to take part in the battle from its inception. He was given command of the 7th Panzer Division. This was made up of the 25th Panzer Regiment and the 37th Panzer Reconnaissance Battalion, as well as three motorized infantry units, the 6th and 7th Rifle Regiments and the 7th Motorcycle Battalion; an engineer battalion; and two regiments of artillery, the 78th Field Artillery Regiment (three battalions of three four-gun batteries) and the 42nd Anti-Tank Artillery Battalion. As a whole the 7th was regarded as a 'light' division and it had been constituted only during the winter. Instead of the normal two tank regiments, it had only one though this was three rather than two battalions strong. It also had 60 fewer tanks than other divisions, 218 instead of the usual 278 and of these more than half were the Czechoslovak light-medium T-35 and T-38s.

The reason for this comparative weakness was that the role of the 7th Panzer and its sister unit, the 5th Panzer, was regarded as supportive. The main thrust was to be made by a Panzer Group under Field Marshal von Kleist consisting of two corps. This was to be the spearhead of List's Twelfth Army. Of these two corps, one, Guderian's, was to strike near Sedan and the second, under Reinhardt, was to cross the river at Monthermé. The 5th and 7th Panzer Divisions, making up Hoth's Panzer Corps, were to provide flank cover for these and were given the objective of crossing the Meuse at points between Givet and Namur.

Rommel did not arrive at 7th Division's headquarters at Bad Godesberg until 15 February, for the time being leaving Lucie and Manfred at Wiener Neustadt.

Left: German soldiers pictured during the 'Phony War.' The banners ask the French troops across the border why they are fighting.

Weeks of rich living and inactivity spent in Hitler's retinue had left him feeling inert and flabby and, in preparation for what was to come, he set about getting himself back in trim with physical exercise. At Bad Godesberg he decided that many of his fellow officers would benefit from something similar, but, as he wrote to Lucie, he found a notable lack of enthusiasm on their part for joining him in such activities as early morning jogging sessions round the neighboring countryside.

Right: General Guderian pictured in his command vehicle during the Battle of France.
Below: German and Czech-built tanks of a Panzer division at rest. A Storch reconnaissance aircraft flies overhead.

Right: The ruins of Sedan where the Germans made their most important breakthrough in May 1940.

At the same time, he realized he was a newcomer to armored warfare and had to spend much of his time absorbing its basic theory and practice. All this had, however, to be fitted in with his main task of divisional training. He was already developing ideas which were tested out in exercises conducted across the country. They included fast movement in formations of varying size, gunnery and radio-operation practice. They were long days and, though he liked to get to bed early, it was rare for him to do so before 2300 hours because of paper work which needed to be completed.

He had, of course, gathered a new group of subordinates round him and of these undoubtedly the one who was closest to him was Colonel Karl Rothenburg, a 44-year-old, former police officer, and winner of the *Pour le Mérite*. He was to command the 25th Panzer Regiment and in the forthcoming battle, Rommel

was to owe him his life on many occasions.

On 10 May, along a line from the north of Holland to the Maginot Line, the assault began. To the delight of the German planners, the British and French did just what was expected of them and left their fortified frontier positions to help Dutch and Belgian troops tottering under the onslaught.

That day the 7th Panzer Division began crossing at a point about 30 miles south of Aachen. In fact its own advance, like that of all the armored forces in Army Group A was virtually unopposed. The Belgian road blocks were desperately undermanned and the French cavalry scouts sent to reconnoiter could not get close enough to make an accurate assessment of the size of the advancing horde. Rommel's unit also had its first brush with enemy armor. It had already been discovered and widely broadcast by the French propaganda that German antitank shells often just bounced off the 40–60 mm steel plating of the best French tanks. As an answer to this, Rommel had urged his units to drench with fire any area they suspected of being enemy held as they approached it and before their adversary knew what was happening. These tactics paid dividends here as they were to do later and the French retreated without a struggle. 'The day,' as Rommel wrote, 'goes to the side that first

Left: Rommel (right) with General Hoth who commanded XV Panzer Corps which included Rommel's 7th Panzer Division.

plasters its opponents with fire.'

On 14 May they came to the first physical barrier – the River Meuse near Dinant. Here units of Corap's Ninth Army had built a strong defensive line where they fought doggedly. There were no bridges and assault boats were sunk as soon as they were launched. Attempts were made to build pontoons under fire, Rommel throwing himself into the labor and thereby earning fresh plaudits from his troops. However, it was French

Above: The Char B was among the most powerful tanks in operation in 1940. However, the commander, alone in the turret, had to operate the 47mm gun and take tactical decisions.
Below: Rommel took this photograph of the tanks of his division advancing.

negligence which allowed the enemy to cross. A weir had been left intact by demolition squads and men from Rommel's motorcycle infantry unit drove across in single file, established a small lodgment, which had been enlarged sufficiently by the next morning to allow tanks to start crossing.

In this way the 7th Division became the first German unit to cross the Meuse. It was, as Sir Basil Liddell Hart points

Below: German infantry on the march. Apart from the panzer divisions few German units had motor transport for their men.

out, a vital achievement, especially in its effects on the French Ninth Army commander. He was, of course, being threatened at several points along his river line, although it was only at Dinant that this had become an actual breach. As is usually the case with armies when shock and defeat are so inextricably mixed, panic rumor massively exaggerated the danger and, instead of using his forces to stop the Dinant gap, he ordered a wholesale retreat westward which had the effect of making the river crossing easier for the attacking forces elsewhere.

That day also brought personal drama

to Rommel. One of his units, advancing out of the Meuse bridgehead, appeared to have run into trouble and 30 tanks of Rothenburg's 25th Panzer Regiment, which were all that had so far crossed the river, were sent to the rescue, Rommel riding in one of them. It soon transpired that their action was unnecessary. The whole incident had been caused by a mistaken radio signal.

However Rommel's tank had not gone far before it came under heavy French artillery fire and was twice hit, with splinters from one shell injuring Rommel in the face. The driver tried to make for cover and in so doing slid down a steep slope ending up tilted sideways and immobile, within range and visibility of the enemy guns. The only course was to abandon the tank and make a run for it although its commander had just lost his arm and was bleeding profusely. Fortunately their plight was seen by Rothenburg himself who, with guns firing, drove to the rescue.

By 15 May Rommel's division, far in front of the 5th Panzer Division on its right, captured an entire French battery and by next day had burst through fortifications near Clairfay intended as an extension of the Maginot Line. The skirmish which ensued is significant for the reintroduction by Rommel of those tactics he had used so successfully as an infantry commander in World War I. The attack began with artillery fire and smoke, out of which the German tanks burst with guns firing – a contravention of the army order which forbade tanks firing on the move because of the loss of accuracy and consequent waste of ammunition. The psychological effect fully compensated for this and the surprised and terrified defending force, which included armor as well as infantry, was totally overwhelmed.

Rommel's division was still further ahead of its flanking units and its sudden and unexpected appearances led to its being dubbed 'The Ghost Division.' Wherever it did appear it inspired shock and panic. Sometimes it would pass an entire French unit with troops bivouacked and vehicles parked in farmyards or at other points. The mere sight of the black crosses on the Panzers was sufficient to make men throw themselves into ditches or huddle behind hedges, eyes wide with terror. The German units would pass columns of refugees pushing their belongings in pathetic handcarts. They would abandon their burdens and rush for the open fields.

Nevertheless, large-scale mechanized warfare was still a comparatively new thing and if the German command was bolder in its employment than either British or French, they still had misgivings about such overextended advances with open flanks as Rommel was indulging in. He saw things differently and believed that in the new form of war, as in the infantry struggles of the past, surprise was of the essence and its achievement outweighed all other considerations. Taking advantage of the fact that he was beyond radio range of his superiors in the rear, so that his orders could not be countermanded, he swung his unit westward, which is to say toward France, aiming for the River Sambre. The attack began at 0530 hours and within half an hour, Landrécies, on the river's bank was in the hands of the 25th Panzer Regiment and, with it, an intact bridge. Making use of this two of the regiment's battalions, plus part of the motorcycle battalion pushed yet further forward toward Le Cateau, while Rommel went back to bring up the main strength of the division.

By 0730 hours on 17 May the division had advanced almost 50 miles in 24 hours. It was a heady achievement and Rommel, as he declared to a fellow commander, felt as if the old days of mounted warfare, when cavalry had roamed deep into the enemy lines, had returned. He would give axes of advance in terms of major French towns and cities. With Le Cateau in sight his troops were told their next objectives were Arras-Amiens-Rouen-Le Havre, though the last was on the coast in Normandy.

Though the fighting was often hard, divisional casualties totalled 94 with only 34 killed, while the French had lost 10,000 in prisoners alone, as well as 100 tanks and many armored cars and guns. When he was ordered by his superiors to call a halt he would have none of it, persuaded them by his own enthusiasm, and was allowed to press forward.

By 20 May the town of Cambrai, scene of the world's first major tank battle in 1917, had been taken and with it nearly 12,000 enemy troops. The Canal du Nord was crossed at Marcoing and positions taken up round Arras. Again the French frequently found themselves totally surprised and in one case an entire barracks was seized. But, as at Landrécies, the German spearheads had outstripped the follow-up units so far that Rommel was forced to go back personally and hurry them forward.

The weakness of the Allied reaction was not due to lack of troops or tanks. Including the French, British, Dutch and Belgian forces, they had 156 divisions against the Germans' 136. The Allies

Below: The Panzer Mk IV was the best German tank in 1940. The Char B and the Matilda had more armor but poorer overall performance.

also had well over 3000 tanks, organized in 152 battalions compared with the Germans 2800 in their 36 battalions. One reason for the lack of coherence of the Allied response was that few of their tank formations were organized into divisions. No British armored division was fully operational at the start of the battle. Most of the French divisions were designated as light with 200 tanks. The heavy divisions had 150 tanks. Both types of formation compared badly with the 280-tank German divisions. Most of the French armor was even less well placed, being dotted across the land in

Right: A knocked-out British tank in a French town on 27 May 1940. It is an A.9 Cruiser tank armed with a 2-pounder gun and two machine guns.
Left: German tank crewmen inspect an abandoned British light tank near Namur north of where Rommel crossed the Meuse.
Below: Rommel's own photograph of an incident during the German advance. A mine is detonated ahead of a staff car.

small numbers to be used for infantry support.

Despite the strength of their forces, the Anglo-French command had been thrown into utter confusion. The German Army Group A had struck roughly at the point of intersection between Corap's Ninth and Huntziger's Second Army. Huntziger, on the right, had therefore to decide whether to swing his left flank and provide a protective shield for Paris, or his right and join the armies fighting in Belgium. Convinced the French capital was the German objective he took the former course. It was not until 19 May that it was generally realized this had been a miscalculation and the enemy was making for the coast. In fact by his movement Huntziger was actually making their going easier.

Rommel was now moving into the sector of the line held by the small British Expeditionary Force. On 21 May in an effort to disrupt the German advance, they decided to attack the German flank from the Belgian side, in the belief that the French were going to attack from the south. It was a bold attempt. The British forces amounted only to two tank battalions supported by two of infantry. Yet such was the vigor with which the attack was pressed, and the surprise it gave the Germans, that they believed hundreds of British tanks and massive infantry forces were involved. Adding to the panic was the discovery that the British Matilda tanks had armor so thick it could not be penetrated by German tank shells. Alarm spread as far as OKH and a senior staff officer was rushed to Rommel's advanced headquarters. Two Panzer Divisions went as far as to turn about and head for the frontier. However, the British were unable to hold their gains because of lack of infantry and air support, and with the French too hard-pressed to think of attacking, the British pulled back. They had no idea of the terror they had inspired.

One significant aspect of this minor British success was that, besides inflicting far higher casualties on the 7th Panzer Division than the entire campaign had brought so far with 250 killed and prisoners, the cool and accurate gunfire

destroyed at least six German tanks. Rommel himself was very nearly numbered among the dead when an officer at his side was hit while the two of them were standing in the open studying a map.

This skirmish showed how differently the Battle of France might have turned out. Miscalculation about enemy intentions, bad interallied as well as inter-army communications, an inert and top-heavy command structure on the French side, and a lack of organization and discipline consequent upon a demoralization whose roots went deeper than the present conflict, had all combined to undermine the French ability to resist. Rommel's personal achievement lay less in strategic skill than in his intuitive recognition of the enemy's condition and in his ability to take full advantage of it.

Right: Rommel is pictured here immediately after he was presented with the Knight's Cross of the Iron Cross.

Left: The harbor at Dunkirk is partially blocked by sunken ships while wrecked and abandoned British equipment covers the quay.

However he had taken inordinate risks and a determined enemy had shown it was possible to make him pay dearly for them. It was only lack of sufficient strength at the psychological moment which prevented the cost from being still greater. (The British success at Arras was not, of course, the only example. There were numerous others where French and even the vastly weaker Belgians showed that the German *Blitzkrieg* was far from invincible.)

Perhaps the essential characteristic of a successful commander is the ability to see every success, whatever its true cause, as the outcome of his own genius. Rommel was not deficient in this capacity and his papers are filled with accounts of how every crisis was turned in his own division's favor. Even where, as is frequent, he gives full credit to men and officers he is still by implication praising himself as their leader. There is little doubt, however, that it was by dint of this attitude, and by its development on the French battlefields of 1940, that the confidence necessary for the great North African victories was built up.

All the same, if the advance continued after the Battle of Arras, he was well aware of being under constant harassment. On 22–23 May the River Scarpe was crossed, but Mont St Eloi, overlooking it, was captured only after a struggle in which it was once retaken by the French. By 26 May bridgeheads had been secured on the La Bassée Canal at points on either side of Guinchy. On 27 May Rommel was awarded the Knight's Cross, the first divisional commander to be so honored. That same day, Hoth gave him temporary command of the 5th Panzer Division so that the two might act in unison in the assault on the industrial city of Lille.

In the next 48 hours there occurred another of those incidents which indicated that he had a charmed life. A signals error led to German shells falling on a temporary divisional headquarters. Rommel and the commander of a reconnaissance battalion made a dash for the radio van to get the bombardment stopped and in the process the latter was killed.

By the 29th his forces were in a blocking position across the main road west of Lille and helped to trap nearly half the French First Army. The French units fought with the greatest bravery in an effort to tie down German forces which might otherwise have been used to dislocate the evacuation from Dunkirk, but were forced to surrender on the 31st. They were accorded full honors of war and there is a picture of German officers saluting as the Lille defenders marched past them with fixed bayonets.

Rommel's division was then pulled out of the line for a brief rest. On 2 June he was visited by Hitler and his letter to Lucie next day had him rhapsodizing about it and how he was ordered to accompany the Führer on the rest of his front-line tour, 'the only divisional commander who did.' Since Goebbels, the Propaganda Minister, liked to project successful generals to the public as if they were film stars, Rommel was now

Below: The beach near Dunkirk on 4 June 1940. Trucks were often used to form temporary piers during the evacuation.

something of a national hero and he asked Lucie to cut out all the newspaper articles about him so that he could study them later.

As he said in his letter to her on 29 May, the Battle of France was now about to reach its last act. Holland and Belgium were already out of the struggle and groaning under Nazi occupation. The French had lost 30 divisions and the 66 left were mostly under strength and stretched along a front longer than the original, prewar one. The 12 divisions of the British Expeditionary Force had successfully escaped via Dunkirk only by abandoning all their heavy equipment so that their value as fighting units was nil. Only two British divisions remained in France with two more, half trained on their way.

The French had demonstrated their

desperation when, on 20 May, General Maxime Weygand, already 73, was summoned from command of their forces in the Levant to supersede Gamelin in overall command of the Allied armies. His first action was to cancel the only concerted offensive action his predecessor had ordered – an attack from both sides on the German column advancing toward the coast.

On 5 June the three German army groups swung southwards. On 6 June Rommel's 7th Panzers were over the Somme. On the 7th they advanced 30 miles, in the process splitting the French Tenth Army holding the sector from Amiens to the Channel. By the 9th they were on the Seine, 10 miles from Rouen. Next day they reached the sea west of Dieppe.

After the struggle through the dusty

summer roads and fields, the sight of water was magical. Rommel records how he and his men climbed from their vehicles and walked down the shingle until the sea lapped their boots. Some men even began wading out fully dressed and had to be called back. Rothenburg, the 25th Panzer Regiment commander, drove his tank right to the water's edge.

Yet the fighting was not completely over. At St Valéry, along the coast, a combined Anglo-French force was awaiting evacuation and Rommel wanted to prevent this. Although every attempt to embark was interdicted by the German artillery, the defenders held out with their British commander, General Fortune, rejecting the German surrender demand. Rommel was particularly impressed by a Royal Navy commander who stood out in the open, within range

Below: French plans in 1940 depended too heavily on fixed defenses.

of the German machine guns, as he urged the men about him to carry on the fight. Asked later by a German officer if he did not feel himself to blame for the heavy casualties sustained in a futile action, he answered him in German, 'Would you have acted differently?'

However, despite efforts of this kind, by the 12th the outskirts of St Valéry were reached and when a last desperate attempt to embark the troops failed with serious losses to the Royal Navy, the garrison was compelled to give in. Twelve thousand prisoners were taken, the 8000 British captives including Fortune himself – 'a particular joy to us,' Rommel says. He was, however, surprised by the sang-froid of the British officer prisoners who 'stalked around laughing' in front of the house in which they had been caught. Nonetheless, when their captors invited them to dinner, they firmly declined. Other prisoners taken included the commander of the French IX Corps, while, in addition, masses of booty fell into German hands.

In the following days the 7th Panzer Division began advancing up the Cotentin Peninsula in Normandy with the great port of Cherbourg as its objective. Once more, it found itself confronting a determined defense whose ferocity increased as the distance to the city decreased. The French troops held out from well-chosen positions and each of these had to be reduced before further progress was possible. In the late afternoon and early evening of 18 June two of the hills overlooking the city were taken and Rommel's troops then began advancing into the suburbs. It was not until the following day, when the divi-

Above left: British and French prisoners march into captivity near St Valéry. The German looking on is probably from one of Rommel's tank units.

Top: Rommel with Major General Fortune of the British 51st (Highland) Division. Fortune and many of his men were captured in St Valéry.

Above: Rommel issues orders for the advance to continue from St Valéry while captured French officers wait in the background.

sional artillery had come up, that the city was finally subjugated and the French surrendered with 30,000 men falling prisoner. However the British troops had been able to escape, though only by the skin of their teeth.

Rommel himself almost failed to see the end of the struggle. As he was passing through the town of Flers, he came upon a group of French civilians and troops. They appeared as cowed as such groups had on other occasions when suddenly a civilian detached himself from the crowd and ran toward Rommel brandishing a revolver. He owed his life to the French troops who grabbed the man and disarmed him before he could shoot.

But beyond that sector of the battlefield where Rommel and his division were locked in struggle events were moving with ever-quickening tempo. Paris, declared an open city to spare it the ravages of war, had been occupied and the government moved to Bordeaux. On the 16th the prime minister, the indomitable Paul Reynaud, had resigned in favor of the 84-year-old Marshal Philippe Pétain, named 'the Hero of Verdun' after his epic defense of the fortress there in 1916. He had been saying for days that his first act should he become premier would be to seek an armistice.

On the 19th, the day on which the 7th Panzer Division seized Cherbourg, Germany announced its readiness to present terms. Rommel's prediction of 29 May had proved all too accurate.

As for Rommel himself, he had gone into the struggle an untried armor commander and emerged with a scintillating reputation. One reason for this was his boundless, Napoleonic energy and, like the Frenchman who had always been his hero, he seemed to need only brief catnaps to restore his vital forces. A more important reason was his instinctive comprehension of the way in which battles were now to be fought. His method of command was unorthodox, as his son Manfred remarked, but was ideally suited to the situation of a fast-moving battle. He led his men from the front and was always in the thick of the conflict – a characteristic which did not escape their observation. His bold tactics of advancing with all speed and without consideration of flank danger, though they had often petrified his superiors, had been amply justified by results.

Above: Marshal Pétain led the government which negotiated the surrender.

Another reason for his success had been his flair for improvisation. He had, for example, introduced the principle of 'line of thrust' as a means of delineating his movement. Before each advance, two points were designated and all subsequent positions given in relation to them. Thus if artillery support was needed at a certain place, the gunner officers were simply sent a radio message giving the point along the line of thrust. He also took to signposting his route so that follow-up units could locate him. This was quite contrary to instruction since it could also act as a means of informing the enemy of his whereabouts, but it prevented confusion.

All in all, he could feel that not only had he acquired glory for himself and his unit, but he had advanced his own career by solid achievement.

Seen from a British perspective, the period following the Fall of France was one replete with life and death drama. No sooner were the last troops back from Dunkirk than the skies were filled with the enemy bombers and the Battle of Britain joined. Seen from a European perspective, it was a time of waiting. The French, Dutch, Belgians and Norwegians were getting used to the presence of occupying enemy troops and for many Germans, especially for soldiers like Rommel, there seemed to be nothing to do other than wait for the next climax which was expected to be the invasion of Britain.

As we have seen, Rommel had already

Right: The crew of a four-wheeled armored car survey the empty boulevards of Paris immediately after the occupation.

become the darling of the German Press. In August he was collaborating with Goebbels in the production of the film *Sieg im Westen* (*Victory in the West*), a record of events from 10 May 1940. Unlike the other belligerents the Germans had no war correspondents, by decree of the propaganda minister. Instead the struggle was covered by the men of the Propaganda Kompanien, who were normal members of the armed forces, who were also accredited to the ministry as writers, photographers, broadcasters or movie cameramen. They reported directly from the front line. It was this which gave the amazing sense of actuality to German reporting of the conflict, at least in its early stages. Thousands of feet of film had been shot during the Battle of France and by no means all had been shown on the *Wochenschau* or weekly newsreels. It was still felt that some highlights ought to be reenacted and, back on his former battlefields,

Left: A German 37mm antitank gun outside the Gare de l'Est in Paris. A gendarme looks on.

Rommel found himself playing the roles of both star and director of many of the sequences. He appears to have enjoyed it enormously.

The propaganda minister was one of those party leaders with whom Rommel had become acquainted on those occasions when he found himself attached to the Führer's entourage, and he was much too shrewd and ambitious not to realize the benefits of keeping the friendship in good repair. Goebbels, for his part, saw the stocky Swabian as the personification of the National Socialist soldier who represented a break with the aristocratic past.

Just before the 7th Panzer Division went to France Goebbels gave Rommel a camera. Pictures he took with it are still in circulation. Many found their way into a family album, but some were used in a special feature in the *Frankfurt Illustrierter Zeitung*, a popular picture magazine.

Rommel, it could be said, had more than just a flair for getting into the headlines. He made sure he was on good terms with members of the Propaganda Kompanien assigned to him. Later he was to claim that this was because he knew the demoralizing effect his name had on the enemy and liked to make sure they were constantly made aware of his presence.

An example of his attitude to Propaganda Kompanien members is shown in his treatment of Karl Hanke. This man, later to become an infamous Nazi Gauleiter in Silesia, was an official in Goebbels's ministry before being sent to Rommel's staff. In order to curry favor with him, Rommel actually offered him command of a tank company before the assault on St Valéry, though his army rank was only lieutenant and he had no relevant experience whatsoever. In the upshot Hanke so mishandled his vehicles that he needed help from Rothenburg. Nonetheless, Rommel recommended him for the Knight's Cross, sending the recommendation direct to Hitler, thus ignoring normal army channels. However, when only hours later Hanke offended him by suggesting that his own influence with the party was such that he could have even a general dismissed,

Above: Goebbels was probably the most able of Hitler's henchmen. Early in his career Rommel cultivated good relations with him.

Rommel dispatched a messenger to intercept the citation. This incident, which became widely known, cost Rommel considerable popularity.

In those early days of the war, it is plain that the only reason for Rommel to treat the Nazi Party and Propaganda Ministry officials with such deference was because he saw in them the medium through which he could keep himself before the eyes of Berlin. He ensured this in other ways, too. After his greatest successes, he would send Hitler a personal copy of his battle dispatch. On another occasion he sent an album of photographs, most of them taken with the camera Goebbels had given him. He was delighted when he was told that Hitler had actually looked through them.

It is said that it was at this time that Rommel began to incur the active jealousy of the army's 'old guard' who despised all self-publicizing on the part of officers. Snobbery, of course, came into it – but then Rommel always found snobbery in any situation in which he came off worse. For all that, his critics deserve a little sympathy. There is no doubt that he falsified accounts of the French campaign in order to enhance the role played in it by his 7th Panzers, for example, by making it look as if neighboring units were making slower progress

Left: German troops form up for the Paris victory parade.

than they actually were. He also ignored the contribution made to victory by other arms of the services, notably the Luftwaffe for which he had hardly a good word to say.

In some cases, he even claimed for himself successful operations carried out by entirely different formations, and more than one critic at the time and subsequently has pointed out that Rommel's division took heavier casualties than others because of the ruthless and sometimes thoughtless and impulsive way in which he pushed it forward. In any event, it was also true that however brilliant a divisional commander he was, his ability to influence the total outcome was, by definition, limited and it must have been peculiarly galling to other

Above: German soldiers at ease in Paris. Such pictures were excellent material for the German propaganda machine.

generals to see newspapers and cinema screens making it seem that Rommel alone had won the campaign.

It may or may not have been because of this that his promotion to lieutenant general was delayed. Certainly he believed that headquarters' jealousies were responsible and did not hesitate to say so. Whatever others might have been saying or thinking about him, he was more popular than ever with the younger German officers, young men bred in the Hitler Youth and deeply indoctrinated with National Socialism, who saw him as their example.

4:NORTH AFRICA

Sieg im Westen completed and distributed, Rommel returned to his division practicing for Operation Sea Lion, the invasion of Britain. By mid-September, however, it was clear that the Luftwaffe and not the Royal Air Force was being driven from the skies and that without adequate air cover to guard the invasion fleet the whole venture was far too hazardous.

As early as 6 September and again on the 26th, Admiral Raeder, the Navy Commander in Chief, proposed an alternative strategy. In North Africa Mussolini was nursing inflated visions of conquest. Raeder was candidly doubtful that the Italians could achieve them on their own. On the other hand, for the British, the Mediterranean was the 'pivot of their world empire.' If Germany threw her lot in with the Italians the seizure of the Suez Canal might easily be encompassed with further rich prizes lying beyond in Palestine, Syria and Turkey.

Raeder was absolutely right in his assessment. Britain's position in the Middle East was extremely precarious while, at the same time, she depended on the oil wells of the region for both power for industry and the fuelling of the Royal Navy. In the spring of 1939 there had been joint French and British discussion on the security of the area and, on the British side, one result was that Lieutenant General Sir Archibald Wavell was appointed Commander in Chief, Middle East, in August 1939. He established his headquarters in Cairo.

Then 55, Wavell was regarded as a highly competent, though personally somewhat shy and taciturn officer. He had spent a large part of his military career in the area, having served as a liaison officer with the Russian Imperial Army in the Caucasus in 1916, later as a member of Allenby's staff in the war with Turkey, and in 1937 as commander of the British forces in Palestine. However, the fall of France had thrown the defense of the entire region onto his own slender forces.

In Libya these comprised Lieutenant General Richard O'Connor's Western Desert Force, later to become the Eighth Army. Its 30,000 troops included the 7th Armored Division (later nicknamed 'The Desert Rats') and the 4th Indian Division, though he was to receive some reinforcements subsequently including Australian, New Zealand and South African troops. For all this weakness, the only response Raeder's plan drew from the Reich Chancellery was a polite indication of interest from Hitler's aides.

The truth was that Hitler was beginning to nurse an even more inflated vision of his own, one which would extend the 1000-year Reich far east to the Urals. Thirty-six years earlier, Germany's then Supreme War Lord, Kaiser Wilhelm II, had declared that the Czar's empire was in the mood of 'a sick tom cat.' His successor seemed to take a similar view of post-revolutionary Russia. The whole edifice was rotten and only a kick at the front door would bring it to collapse, he claimed.

Autumn passed into winter and apart

Below: Hitler and Mussolini, uneasy partners in the fighting in North Africa.

Left: A classic image of the desert war; Australian troops fire a 25-pounder gun, the standard British field artillery weapon.

Left: General Wavell (right), the British Commander in Chief, and General O'Connor who led Western Desert Force to its first victories over the Italians.

from discussions and the passing to and fro of memoranda, often forgotten even by their authors as quickly as they were written, nothing concrete happened. The most obvious conclusion is that surprise at the defeat of the Luftwaffe had caught the Germans unprepared and its ruler simply did not know what to do next. However, there was considerable activity in one sphere. Throughout the newly occupied territories, west and east, anti-Semitic programs were being implemented and behind closed doors, within the highest enclaves of state and party, the first tentative steps were being taken toward the 'Final Solution,' the planned extermination of the Jews of Europe.

The delay on the war front was leading to a loss of advantage to Germany. For one thing the RAF's victory had not escaped the notice of the occupied peoples. The increasing confidence in the island-fortress gave them the will to slough off the apathy of the vanquished and renew the fight when they could.

As to the problem of North Africa,

this was solved by events themselves. In September 1940 the Italian Tenth Army, totalling nearly 250,000 under Marshal Graziani, began crossing the Egyptian frontier. The Western Desert Force fought a defensive battle through the autumn, but on 9 December in the first major British offensive of World War II, they went over to the attack. In the ensuing weeks the Italians were driven back across the Western Desert through Cyrenaica. By February Wavell's 30,000 had advanced 500 miles and taken 130,000 prisoners, and they had not yet stopped. Total catastrophe faced Mussolini, the Italian dictator, and there is little doubt that had the British advantage been pushed to the ultimate, his régime would have toppled.

But there was a purely physical limit to what so small a force could achieve, especially when short of equipment and with supply lines attenuated to breaking point. In particular, there was concern over fuel supplies. All this Hitler quite rightly divined. The enemy, he believed, was incapable of large-scale exploits for the time being, though the Italians, their nerve shattered by the past six weeks, found it hard to convince themselves this was so. It followed from Hitler's view,

that quite small German forces could stop any further British incursions. On 10 February he wrote offering the Italian dictator German assistance and this was gratefully accepted.

In concrete terms what he had in mind was to send the 5th Light Division, less its 5th Panzer Regiment, as reinforce-

Above: German troops parade before Rommel and General Gariboldi immediately after arrival in Africa in February 1941.
Below: Italian prisoners taken during the first British offensive against the Italians. The Beda Fomm battle, planned by O'Connor, is widely regarded as a masterpiece of generalship.

ment. Major General Johannes Streich, who now commanded 5th Light had been commander of the 15th Panzer Regiment, part of the 5th Panzer Division, which had come temporarily under Rommel's direction during the attack on Lille. They had argued fiercely when Streich accused Rommel of misreading maps – which, as it happened, was true. It was ironical, therefore, that the former commander of the 7th Panzer Division should also have been going to Africa. The two remained thoroughly antipathetic to one another and their quarrels were to continue. Now, having at last been promoted to lieutenant general, Rommel was given the title of Commander in Chief, German Forces in Libya, though his brief was to be one simply of assessment of the military situation.

Below: German Mk III tanks parade through a coastal town soon after their arrival in Africa. They are armed with 37mm guns.

There was still another irony. In the summer of 1940 after the fall of France, a friend, Kurt Hesse, had mentioned to Rommel that he had heard rumors that the German army was to be thrown into North Africa to save the Italians. Rommel insisted he had it on the Führer's own authority that 'not a man or a penny-piece' was to be expended there. Hesse appeared profoundly relieved by this assurance.

In a short letter to Lucie, he explained that he could not tell her where he was going, but that it was a place which ought to benefit his rheumatism. This had first set in in France and the doctor treating it had commented that he should find a way of getting himself posted to Africa. Accordingly, Lucie reading this was not too hard put to divine where he had gone.

He actually arrived two days after Hitler's letter to Mussolini, having de-

German archeologist on his staff.

At the time of his arrival the Italian army was in retreat toward Tripoli and, though they were not yet pursued by the British, they were very pessimistic about their chances of holding the city.

On the afternoon of his arrival, Rommel decided to overfly the area. Two days later, as his first troops began disembarking, he posted them to a defense line well to the east, nearer to the advancing British than the line Bastico had been contemplating. However, he had no illusions about his ability to hold if the attack came in strength and without consideration of casualties.

He had been accompanied on his flight of inspection by the man whose influence with Hitler was probably greater than anybody's: Hitler's personal adjutant, Colonel Rudolf Schmundt. Schmundt returned to Germany to report that the new commander in Libya was tackling his job with customary energy, but required men and material if he was to keep the British out of Tripoli. As a result of this intervention, it was agreed that the 5th Panzer Regiment should be released to the 5th Light Division and, in addition, the 15th

cided in his own mind that he was going to ignore formalities and take overall command. After this decision the African theater was dominated by the Germans even though Rommel was technically subordinate to the new Italian commander, General Bastico, whom he promptly christened 'Bombastico' and though there were actually far more Italian troops present (at one time the number approached a quarter of a million).

Northwest Africa is mountainous, but Libya and Egypt, where most of the coming struggle was to take place, is largely desert. Much of this is rocky, stony wasteland where nothing grows, but it is interspersed with the sandy stretches which form most people's idea of desert. One of the first questions confronting Rommel was, indeed, whether motor vehicles could actually use the terrain at all and it was finally discovered it was possible if tire pressures were reduced to give adequate grip.

There are few railroads and not many paved roads. Such as there were, were mostly along the coastal strip connecting the small townships.

The towns appeared much as they must have done in Roman times: dusty streets with flat-roofed, usually single-storied white-washed houses glowing in the sun and the only greenery coming from clumps of agave or tall palm trees.

In some towns, like Tripoli, a series of conquerors had left their mark by erecting buildings in their own national idiom and that of their era. Arab bazaar areas gave most of them an exotic quaintness to western eyes and this was enhanced by the laden camels or donkeys evident in the streets. Rommel, for his part, never gave the slightest indication of interest in the area or its history, though he was said to have developed a sort of dilettante preoccupation with archeology largely as a result of having a

Below: Rommel on the lookout. Behind is an Italian M13/40 tank. It carried a 47mm gun and was the best of the poor Italian tanks.

Above: A revealing comparison: the Italian light tank is dwarfed by the German armored car with its 75mm gun.

Panzer Division should also be sent as soon as possible. It was these two divisions which made up the Deutsche Afrika Korps or DAK and Rommel was appointed their commander, though, in fact, he retained the more resplendent title of Commander in Chief, German Forces in Libya. Even with the 5th Panzer Regiment his strength was still below that of his enemy, if he discounted the Italian forces, which, in fact were poorly equipped and whose tanks the troops called 'mobile coffins.'

Rommel reckoned he would need two weeks free of enemy interference to make his line secure. Granted this he challenged them to attack Tripoli, but in the meantime for the benefit of the panicky Italians and, above all, for British air reconnaissance he endeavored to make his forces appear much greater than they were by every trick of camouflage.

However, the British were themselves

Below: Italian infantry advance past a German Mk III tank. Note the pile of stores carried on the engine deck of the tank.

hostage to events in the war at large. Besides his ill-starred North African adventure, Mussolini had embarked on an invasion of Greece. Despite Greek success in dealing with the Italian threat unaided and worries that intervention might well bring the Germans in, a British and Anzac force was sent to Greece. The nearest and indeed the only source was Wavell's army which was depleted for the purpose. (The sole result was the one the Greeks had feared: the Germans entered the war and the British contingent was too small to redress the balance. Greece was occupied and the North African campaign irretrievably weakened.) The Western Desert Force was weaker at that moment for other reasons, too. Its finest unit, the 7th Armored Division, was judged in need of rest and refitting after its battle with the Italians and was sent to Egypt. With it had gone the force commander, O'Connor, whose place was taken by General Sir Philip Neame, an officer totally lacking in desert experience. The 9th Australian Division had taken over from the

6th, but only half of its strength was immediately available owing to equipment maintenance difficulties. These risks had all been taken in the belief that the Germans would be unlikely to hazard their own forces in a venture with the collapsing Italian army.

The British problems were not immediately known to Rommel, but on 4 March Streich's 5th Light Division reached Mugtaa unopposed and established itself along a front nearly 500 miles east of Tripoli. Even the Italians could sense a new confidence abroad – Rommel's dynamism was infectious. The Italians also observed the tight discipline he enforced on his men and especially his officers which contrasted with the easy-going laxity of the Italian army. He would arrive at outposts early in the morning, often taking their commanders by surprise and delivering a reprimand if they were not up and about like himself. He would even check minor details and always insisted that his own instructions were obeyed to the letter. Where there was failure, he

would be blistering while also explaining why such instructions were necessary.

Also in contrast with the Italian officers, whom he considered overweight from ·too much good living, his own existence was as frugal as always. He did not smoke. He seemed not to notice what food was put before him and only drank on those occasions when a measure of sociability was called for, as on a fellow officer's birthday when he would take a single glass of wine.

If there was any intoxicant in his life it was that of ambition. By mid-March he was dreaming of an advance to the Nile and had already boasted to the audience at a special screening of *Sieg im Westen* in Tripoli that it would shortly be seeing and perhaps participating in a film to be called *Sieg in Afrika*.

Back in Berlin on the 19 February, he was decorated with the Oak Leaves by Hitler, but found the Army General Staff unwilling to back the schemes he had in mind which, naturally enough, would require further and more substantial reinforcement. He supposed them to be shortsightedly unimpressed by the potential of North Africa. The real reason was that they were finalizing plans for the invasion of the USSR and every available man and tank was spoken for.

Above: Rommel watches an artillery barrage take effect from his half-track command vehicle 'Greif.' Rommel liked to be close to the fighting.

However he returned to Africa with his vision undimmed and ordered an advance still further east, to Mersa Brega. This was in strict contravention of orders from Berlin and Rome. The Italians, who were after all providing the greater part of forces involved, even if they played the less substantial role, wanted no offensive until the end of May by which time the 15th Panzer Division would have arrived. All the same, the British were forced to withdraw from positions they had only just reached. An exultant Rommel decided to exploit success and push on to Agedabia, the next town on the coast, which fell on the afternoon of 2 April.

Tripoli was safe, but he was unsatisfied. His next orders were for an advance across the center of Cyrenaica with the Egyptian frontier as its ultimate goal. His officers were incredulous at such an improvised advance across the open desert. Streich expressed his own misgivings so openly that Rommel resolved to have him removed at the first opportunity.

These doubts were shared by the Italians. The disaster-prone Graziani had been replaced by Italo Gariboldi, a plump, avuncular officer with a bristling white moustache and a northern Italian's forthrightness. On 3 April he arrived at Rommel's headquarters and ordered him to stop all further advance. Rommel was at first placatory, since he rather liked Gariboldi, but he finally lost his temper and there was a long and bitter quarrel. The Italian seemed to have won the day when, in the early evening, a signal came from OKH which confirmed that present lines were to be held. Rommel did not, however, show this to his guest and instead declared that it was a directive giving him 'complete freedom of action' and indeed even went so far as to write to Lucie giving it the same sense that night.

His plan was to cross the Cyrenaican desert with his forces divided into three columns. One was to advance along the coast road, one across the base of the Peninsula and the third was to bisect it about halfway up. The defenders would, it was hoped, be caught in the area between the three prongs. Bastico's fury was not allayed even when the coast column reported the seizure of Benghazi whose earlier fall to Wavell had caused such consternation to the Italians. Anger at Rommel's insubordination spread to

Below: An Italian Macchi MC.200 fighter plane. These machines were underpowered and poorly armed. Airpower was vital during the desert campaigns particularly in the struggle for control of the Mediterranean supply routes.

Below: Rommel and the Italian General Gariboldi at the first Afrika Korps parade in Tripoli.

Berlin where it was suspected, perhaps not entirely without justice, that having had his schemes thwarted, he was enlarging the scope of the battle by his own actions, as others had done in the past and were to do in the future, knowing that if he was successful, the pressure of public opinion would make it hard to deny him the support he needed. Rommel's own defense was that he had had to act before the enemy reinforced or dug himself into impregnable positions.

In any case he refused to halt. He nagged, bullied, threatened and cajoled his subordinates to go on, even when the tanks in Streich's force got themselves stuck in sand drifts and then strayed into a minefield. He had now equipped himself with a Fieseler Storch, a German light observation plane which had the valuable ability of being able to land in a very small area. With this he overflew the entire battle zone. Once, when he saw a motor column stopped for no apparent reason, he dropped a message from the cockpit demanding it move on or he would land to investigate. Sometimes he found himself being shot at by enemy troops; on other occasions it was Italians who mistook his aircraft.

Though they did not come as fast as he wanted, successes were attending his efforts. The day that Benghazi fell, the center column took Msus. The next day the right-hand column took Tengeder in its operations along the base of the peninsula. Then the middle and right-hand columns converged for a combined advance on Mechili. Rommel had been unsure whether to make for Mechili or Tobruk and some units had actually been diverted when he finally decided on Mechili. His attacking forces were dispersed, there were breakdowns from overuse of the tanks and other vehicles and a shortage of fuel. Still he refused to listen to any excuse and, at one point, accused Streich of cowardice, a charge he was forced to retract. Though Rommel took personal control of the operation, the struggle persisted through the 6th and 7th, but the town fell on 8 April in a sandstorm.

He was now more than ever determined on Streich's dismissal and a newcomer to the desert, Major General Heinrich von Prittwitz, was actually given command of the leading troops. However, when Prittwitz was killed on the 10th, Streich was the bearer of the tidings and nearly got himself killed by Rommel's entourage because he used a British car to pursue the general. When reproached for doing this, he told his commander, 'Then, Herr General, you would have killed both your Panzer

division commanders in one day.' Rommel is said to have been rendered silent by this. (Streich finally left in June and was succeeded by Major General Johannes von Ravenstein.)

Though Mechili had not been the 'second Cannae,' promised by Rommel, it had brought in a large bag of prisoners, some 1700, including 70 officers. There was also valuable booty including a British Mammoth command truck which, thereafter, Rommel converted to his own use.

The next stage of the battle was an advance northeast by a detachment under Colonel Ponath to cut off the British escape route out of Derna on the eastern side of the peninsula. In the meantime the coastal column, now itself divided into two, was making toward the same town. British difficulties were increased by the fact that their tanks were also

Below: Rommel's captured Mammoth command truck. Both sides in North Africa made extensive use of captured equipment.

Above: Prisoners taken during Rommel's first offensive. The talented General O'Connor was one important captive.

to persist even after attack upon attack faltered and failed.

Accordingly, he ordered pursuit of the forces he believed to be leaving Tobruk along the coast road, almost unbelievably setting as the final objective the Suez Canal! What he did not yet know was that the British command had ordered that Tobruk be held to the last man in the conviction that it could be sustained and reinforced from the sea. Even as late as mid-April, when it was still unvanquished, Rommel was telling his troops, 'We'll be in Cairo in eight days.'

It may well have been that for the sake of morale he was expressing a confidence he did not actually feel, for the picture

Below: A German 105mm gun bombards Tobruk. In the foreground one of the crew sets the fuse on a shell.

constantly breaking down from overuse and they too had a desperate shortage of fuel. Nonetheless, the German trap round Derna was avoided and a withdrawal to Tmimi successfully carried out, though large numbers of troops fell into Germans hands, among them Generals Neame and O'Connor. O'Connor had largely been responsible for the victories against the Italians only a few weeks before.

The British did have one enormous advantage over their adversaries. Wherever German forces were engaged, they were using the supposedly infallible Enigma coding machine. Cryptographers in Britain had, however, cracked it and were able to listen in to German radio instructions without difficulty. (This sometimes acted against the British, since when orders were received from Berlin, they would expect Rommel to conform and made their own plans accordingly. He frequently confused them by disobedience.)

After Mechili, the Afrika Korps' next objective had to be Tobruk which, if left unsubjugated, would pose a threat to its lines of communication. There is no doubt Rommel expected Tobruk to fall quickly, largely because he was convinced the fortress was in the process of evacuation already, a delusion which was

Above: Rommel with Major General Böttcher who commanded the Afrika Korps artillery very efficiently.

had been sent. Paulus had actually been made lieutenant general in the previous August in advance of his former brother captain, a promotion which had caused some bitter observations from Major General Rommel, about the preferential treatment extended to members of the General Staff.

Rommel at once began bombarding his visitor with demands and complained of supply difficulties. Paulus, very reasonably, pointed out that these were largely of his own making. The nearest substantial port, Tripoli, was now 1100 miles behind the front and it was Rommel's own fault for embarking on this long advance without ensuring he had adequate supply lines.

Paulus was also the recipient of complaints from the men themselves. Many were suffering badly from the heat and felt that not enough had been done to provide them with protection from its ravages. Millions of flies swarmed everywhere, infecting food and causing dysentery and other intestinal diseases. Ironically, their opponents, although they suffered from the depredations of the flies were actually better protected by the use of DDT – invented by a German.

As to the food itself, this was less spartan than plain unhealthy. Fruit and vegetables were unknown and the Germans particularly missed potatoes which at home played such an important part

Below: Sunken ships in Tobruk harbor with smoke rising over the town after an air raid. German airfields were only a few miles away.

which comes to us at this juncture is of a very worried man. He blamed the repeated failures to take Tobruk on the lack of energy of subordinate commanders; he quarrelled with members of his staff and sent some of them home.

On 27 May General Paulus arrived at his headquarters, dispatched from Berlin to carry out an inspection. Paulus was known to Rommel as they had served as captains together in their early army careers and it was for this reason that he

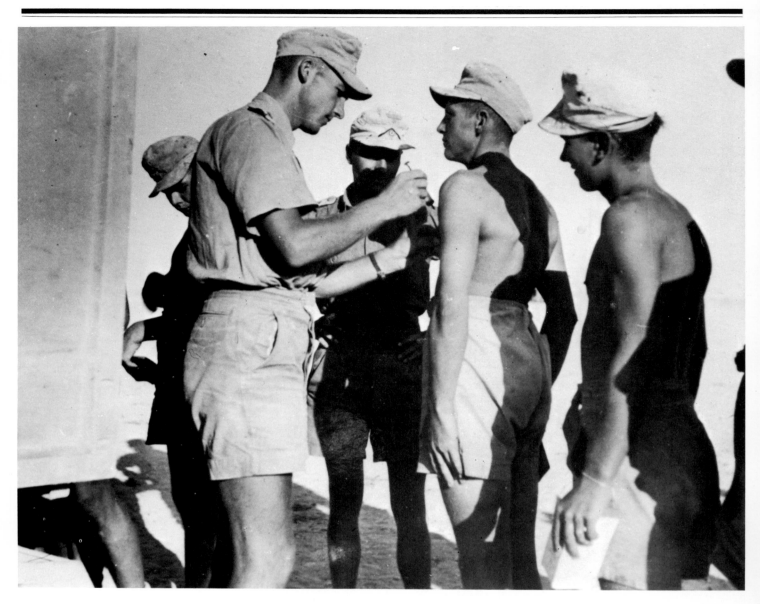

Above: German soldiers line up for innoculations. Rommel, like many of his men, suffered from intestinal diseases.

in their diet. The basic elements of ration were sardines in oil and canned German sausages. As well as this there were small round tins of tough Italian beef which, because the labels were marked 'AM' had been christened *Alter Mann* (Old Man) or, irreverently, 'Ass of Mussolini.' Paulus described these conditions as inhuman and intolerable and said he was going to recommend withdrawal to Gazala where supply lines would be shorter and troops would be able to live in less discomfort.

We know that Rommel took little notice of such recommendations and it has to be said that nowhere were living conditions more austere than at his own headquarters. Such was the shortage of

even such minor luxuries as eggs that one of Rommel's aides was noticed devouring one he was given with such eagerness, while visiting another mess that the senior officer there offered him his own as well. Despite this austerity, Rommel's success was incontestable and it is a tribute to the loyalty he was able to command that his men were prepared to endure such conditions for the privilege of serving under him.

He had retaken Cyrenaica in a matter of weeks and reversed all Wavell's vaunted triumphs. He now stood at the gates of Egypt. Rommel's detractors at OKH could do nothing to prevent Hitler from drawing his own conclusions from these achievements and the propaganda machine from making capital out of them.

By the end of April, although the fortress of Tobruk was still in British hands the Egyptian frontier had been

crossed and on 25 April the mountain pass of Halfaya near the coast had been occupied, but the force which did this was too small to do anything more than consolidate its own position.

The loss of the pass was important to the British all the same, as it would allow the Germans, once they had amassed the necessary strength, to debouch on to the Egyptian plains with Cairo and Suez within range. Wavell, with his reduced forces, was forced to contemplate counteraction, which took the form of a short offensive, Brevity. This began on 15 May

Above right: A German officer negotiates the purchase of some fresh food. Chickens and eggs were among the few commodities available to supplement the ration issue.
Right: A German 37mm antitank gun in a mountain position. Defenses like this were established at Halfaya after its capture.

and had sufficient initial success to send a frisson of horror down the spines of OKH in Berlin. Anxious at the dispersal of Rommel's units, they ordered him to concentrate toward the Egyptian frontier in the vicinity of Sollum, leaving the investment of Tobruk to the Italians. By the second day the British were in any case beginning to hesitate. Although their lead units were back in Cyrenaica having taken Fort Capuzzo, this very advance had left them exposed and a German counterattack compelled a withdrawal. The British commanders then seemed to lose heart and ordered a retreat back to Halfaya. (The fighting over this key area was to lead to its being rechristened by the British troops 'Hellfire Pass.')

Halfaya could not, however, be left in enemy hands and on 26 May Rommel threw his forces into an attack on it from both ends, one unit making a sweeping detour deep into the desert in order to get behind it. On 27 May it was regained and measures were taken to strengthen its fortifications.

In mid-May, after a hazardous voyage through the Mediterranean, a British convoy, Tiger, had arrived at Alexandria bringing 43 Hurricane fighters and 238 tanks. With this reinforcement it was possible for Wavell to contemplate a new offensive. It was given the name Battleaxe and the objective of relieving Tobruk.

The plan was for one of the attacking formations, led by a force of Crusader tanks, to sweep across the desert in the general direction of Tobruk, whose garrison was to join in at the right moment. The 11th Indian Brigade, supported by Matilda tanks, would advance on Halfaya simultaneously. What was envisaged in this sector was a purely frontal assault which really meant gambling on the superiority of British tanks and crews over the German defenses.

However, before the attack could begin, tanks and aircraft had to be converted for use in the desert so that the start was delayed until mid-June. When Battleaxe was launched, not only did the Halfaya attackers soon find themselves among the mines and other obstacles concealed to deter just such a venture, but as they pushed on they found themselves contending with another weapon. The

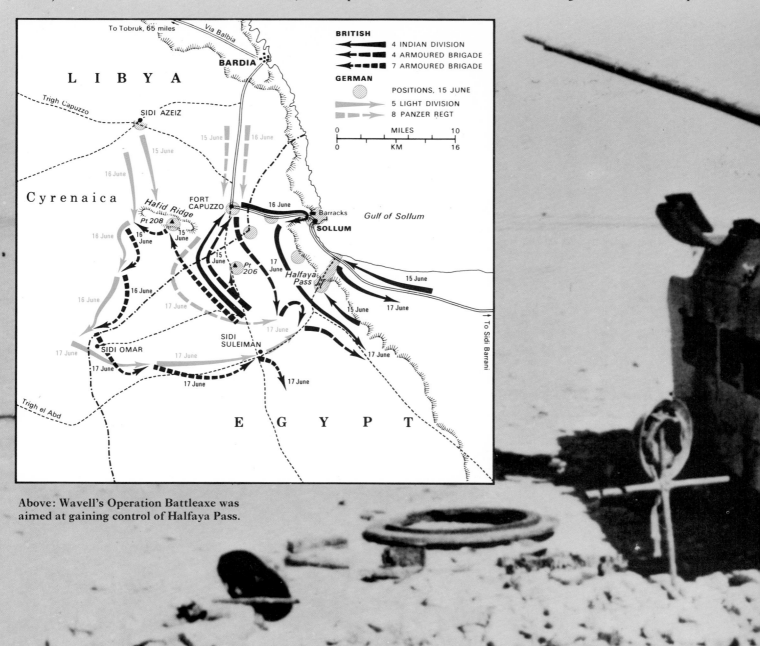

Above: Wavell's Operation Battleaxe was aimed at gaining control of Halfaya Pass.

British Matilda tank, slow moving but extremely heavily armored, had ruled as queen of the battlefield, haughtily impervious to enemy shells, ever since France. In the later stages of the Battle of Arras, however, it had been found that there was one weapon to which it was vulnerable and this was the 88 mm antiaircraft gun which was provided with ammunition and sights for use against armor. Accordingly, Rommel had emplaced batteries of 88s along the Halfaya perimeter.

A British officer taken prisoner in the battle ventured later to suggest that it was a little unfair to use antiaircraft guns against tanks (to which his captor answered it was more than a little unfair to use tanks which nothing less than an

Above: German 88mm guns were emplaced like this at Halfaya Pass at Rommel's orders. When dug in with their barrels only a little above ground they were very difficult to detect and destroy. Below: An abandoned Matilda tank with two of Rommel's officers. The thick armor of the Matilda made it superior to all Axis tanks in 1941 but it could be defeated by the 88. Its 2-pounder gun could only fire armor-piercing ammunition, useless against antitank gun emplacements.

Above: The Germans made good use of
the resources of countries they conquered.
Here a Czech 4.7cm gun is mounted on a
Pz Kw I chassis.

88 mm shell could penetrate). The
officer's remark was itself a tribute to the
success of the gun which, indeed crip-
pled the tank attack and left the infantry
without support. The second attempt to
retake Halfaya Pass failed in this way.

In these circumstances, it would have
been rash of Wavell to press an inland
advance on Tobruk, but the attack in this
sector failed anyway because the Crusader tanks, used for the first time in this
battle, were found to be incapable of
standing up to desert conditions, besides
the damage and destruction wrought on
them by the German mobile forces. At
any rate, a great many broke down. The
entire offensive was called off.

In all Wavell had lost 101 of his 190
tanks – an appalling figure. At the same
time the RAF sacrificed 36 machines.
British army casualties were also higher,
960 to the Axis' 800, but the German and

Italian tank losses were only 12 destroyed
and 50 damaged. Ten Axis aircraft were
lost. The figure for tanks damaged is
significant because the Germans, having
been left masters of the battlefield, were
in a position to recover those capable of
repair while the British had had to
abandon even slightly damaged machines.

The defeat of the Battleaxe offensive
was largely attributable to Rommel's
well-organized defenses and the skill
with which he judged when units could
be moved from one part of the front to
another. This contrasted with the un-
imaginative and sometimes incompetent
conduct of the battle by the British commanders. Rommel let the attackers break
their teeth on his static defenses and only
when this had happened did he send in
his reserves for the kill. It was not, therefore, until the evening of the 15 June that
tanks from the now famous 5th Light
Division came on the scene.

Arriving in the desert at a time of
British ascendancy, Rommel had set

upon the enemy impetuously if successfully. He was by this time getting into his
stride and the edginess of the gambler,
so manifest a few weeks earlier, had now
given place to securely founded confidence. Battleaxe dragged on for three
days, largely because of the obstinacy of
some of the attacking units which continued to give the defenders trouble. It
ended in so complete a vindication of
Rommel that his nominal masters, the
Italians, were forced to applaud and
admit the need to give him adequate
backing for the completion of his task.

One form which the concrete realization of this took was in the building of a
ring road round Tobruk linking with the
coastal highway on either side of the city
which of course remained in British
hands. This would serve the troops
holding the perimeter and investing the
port and would also speed up movement
generally, since it would mean there
would be a continuous, paved road for
traffic to the Egyptian border. The road
was completed by the Italians in three

months – an astonishing feat – and given the name *Achsenstrasse* (Axis-street).

While Rommel was being showered with congratulations, his opponent Wavell was, as might be expected, under a cloud. It was felt he was exhausted and as early as 19 May Churchill had told the Chief of the Imperial General Staff General Dill that he thought Wavell should be sent as Commander in Chief, India, the present incumbent of that position, Claude Auchinleck, replacing him in North Africa. Execution of the decision was delayed until the end of Battleaxe, but on 22 June Wavell and Auchinleck were given the news.

Claude John Eyre Auchinleck was a 54-year-old Northern Irishman, the son of a soldier. He had been educated at Wellington College, a British public school with a markedly military bent. Like Wavell he had served in the Middle East in World War I before going to India as Commander in Chief. A tall, formidable figure, he was in many ways the opposite of his adversary in that he

enjoyed the good things of life and made no secret of the fact. In Cairo he was regarded as something of a socialite, much in demand for bridge parties (a characteristic exploited by German propaganda). He was, for all this, more popular with the troops than the shy and incommunicative Wavell and proved himself a cool and skillful commander, as Rommel was to find and acknowledge, using his armor with far greater understanding than his predecessor. By pure coincidence, the day of his takeover was that on which the Germans launched Operation Barbarossa, the invasion of the USSR.

If the coming weeks could hardly be called a period of inactivity for the troops involved on both sides in the desert, it was one in which the focus of world attention had shifted north and east to the Soviet Union where the Red Army was fighting for survival and looked like succumbing. Among units involved there was the 7th Panzer Division whose fortunes its former com-

Above: The notice-board gives the rules of the road for *Achsenstrasse*.
Below: These German airmen were fortunate to have washing facilities as elaborate as this. Often there was only enough water for drinking and for vehicle radiators.

Left: Digging trenches or gun-pits in the very hard ground around Tobruk meant hours of back-breaking labor.

mander continued to follow with the greatest interest.

Among other things the high summer had seen the fundamental restructuring of the German forces in the theater. Although no complete divisions were sent to Africa until 1942, a number of independent units with their equipment had arrived. These were formed first into the Afrika Division, later renamed 90th Light Division which, though it lacked tanks and was only four battalions strong, was actually well supplied with artillery including three field-gun batteries, an antitank and an 88 mm Flak battalion. At the same time, the 5th Light Division was redesignated the 21st Panzer Division. This meant that German strength amounted to the DAK plus the 90th Light Division and these, together with the Italian XX, XXI and X Corps, mostly outside Tobruk, were constituted in August into a *Panzergruppe Afrika*, of which one-third was German and two-thirds Italian.

Rommel, promoted in the teeth of OKH opposition to a full general, was confirmed in overall command, so rid-ding him of such irritants as his notional subordination to Bastico. However this left his former position as commander of the DAK vacant and two officers held it briefly. The first was Ferdinand Schaal who, already ill on his appointment, never recovered sufficiently to take over. He was succeeded by Philip Müller-Gebhard who had to leave Africa on account of dysentery in mid-September. The sickness which had afflicted these two officers was only a reflection of that suffered by all the German forces and is a measure of the unhealthy conditions under which they were living.

It was not until October that a permanent leader was found in the shape of Lieutenant General Ludwig Crüwell, an officer known to Rommel as he had commanded the 2nd Motorized Division which had been stationed on Rommel's flank during the battle for St Valery.

During this time Rommel was planning an all-out attack to subdue Tobruk, setting the date as 23 November. At the same time Auchinleck was methodically planning his own offensive for the besieged port's relief which was scheduled to begin exactly a week earlier, on the 16th.

In the meantime British raids, often in

Above: Lieutenant General Crüwell took command of the Afrika Korps in October 1941. Like many of Rommel's subordinates he was very able.
Below: German machine gunners move forward. The hard stony ground they are crossing is typical of much of the area over which Rommel's battles were fought.

considerable strength, were carried out far behind the German lines, with the object of harassing communications. Of these the most famous was the so-called Keyes' Raid, the target of which was none other than Rommel himself – a tacit recognition of the impression he had made on the scene.

Named after its leader, Colonel Geoffrey Keyes, the plan was to land commandos from two submarines. They would work their way inland to blow up the villa supposedly used by Rommel and, at the same time, sabotage the Italian headquarters at Cyrene, their intelligence center at Apollonia and disrupt their rear communications. The enterprise was ill-starred from its inception. Weather turned unexpectedly bad; less than half the force got ashore and that far later than intended. However the attack plan was modified on the spot and the prime target, Rommel's Villa, was reached. An attempt to sneak in through the back failed because doors and windows were too heavily secured and the party had to go openly to the front door, knock and burst in as it was opened. This, of course, alerted the occupants and during a short gunfight, Keyes was killed. Charges were placed, but it was found that the fuses, soaked by the incessant rain, would not function.

After using grenades to destroy as much as possible, the party left and successfully reached the evacuation beach. Here the submarine, waiting to take them off, failed to see their signals. In the end all but two of the force were captured. It later transpired that the Arab intelligence on which the raid had been based was faulty. The building assaulted was not one used by Rommel at all and in any case he was at the time in Athens on his way back from a visit to Rome.

In North Africa and in Britain the raid had some effect on flagging morale as demonstrating an ability to strike back and Keyes was awarded a posthumous Victoria Cross, the highest British military decoration. Rommel himself was sufficiently impressed by the daring and courage displayed to send his own chaplain to conduct the burial service of the British officer and the four German soldiers killed in the raid.

On another occasion a raiding party was landed near a beach used by Rommel and his staff for bathing. Two of the raiders were picked up, but the rest disappeared. Always unwilling to have the tenor of life disturbed, the general carried on as usual, but while inspecting trenches near Bardia some days later he and his party were suddenly fired on. They took cover and returned fire with their revolvers and when there was a break made for their cars and drove off. A German patrol which was hurried to the area, searched thoroughly but failed to find any sign of the sniper.

Right: Axis airfields and aircraft were the favorite target for Long Range Desert Group raids.
Below: An LRDG patrol sets out. Such parties caused considerable disruption to Rommel's forces. The patrol uses Chevrolet trucks.

5: THE BRITISH STRIKE BACK

As already noted, Rommel was considering a new offensive scheduled to begin in mid- to late November. He was still dreaming of breaking through to the Suez Canal, an achievement which could shift the course of the war decisively in Germany's favor since Britain, dependent on oil imports from the Arab states via the canal, would then be subjected to a blockade as strangling as that the Royal Navy had imposed on Germany in World War I. However such an ambitious attack required the neutralization of the Tobruk enclave which could menace the German supply lines to an unacceptable extent. Besides Tobruk was a port and its possession would free Rommel from dependence on the more distant harbors of Benghazi and Tripoli.

He had already had to postpone plans to seize it in September for lack of resources. Now that he felt he was strong enough for the attempt his main fear was that the British might forestall him by an attack of their own. He accordingly sent a reconnaissance force deep behind enemy lines and its leaders reported back

that they could find no signs of preparation. All the same, he decided to interpose a protective shield between Tobruk and any British advance from Egypt. He then flew to Rome to explain his plan to Commando Supremo, the Italian headquarters to which he was officially subordinate, and to get their permission for it to be carried out. He allowed himself a day or two extra so that he could celebrate his birthday on the 15th with Lucie and Manfred. He was, of course, on his way back when the Keyes' raid took place.

Notwithstanding the evidence of Rommel's scouts, Auchinleck was making his plans for an offensive with the objective both of relieving Tobruk and recapturing Cyrenaica, though in the opinion of Churchill at a culpably slow pace. What was not appreciated in London, however, was that Auchinleck was dogged by

Right: A British 6-pounder gun recoils after being fired. Like the 2-pounder, it had a good armour-piercing capability but no high-explosive ammunition.
Below: The Suez Canal, seen from a German plane, was a vital lifeline for Eighth Army.

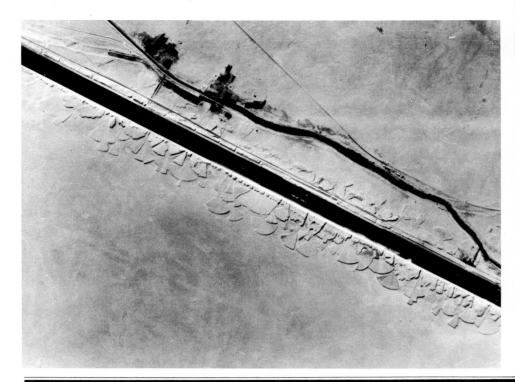

Left: Filling jerry cans at a watering point near El Agheila. The white cross on the cans means that they are for water not gasoline.

problems similar to Rommel's while Rommel had the advantage that he could be supplied through Greece and Italy.

However, on 18 September, the Western Desert Force had been reconstituted into the Eighth Army and put under the command of Lieutenant General Sir Alan Cunningham who had already earned a considerable reputation as a commander in East Africa. Into it was incorporated the garrison of Tobruk – at present, of course under siege – as well as an armored division, three armored brigades and six and a half infantry divisions totalling in all about 188,000 men. These were organized into two corps and an independent brigade group. Their equipment included about 680 tanks as

Below: Rommel's own sketch map of the early stages of the Crusader battles. Rommel's tanks attacked the British forces making for Tobruk but the result was decided by the Allied infantry.

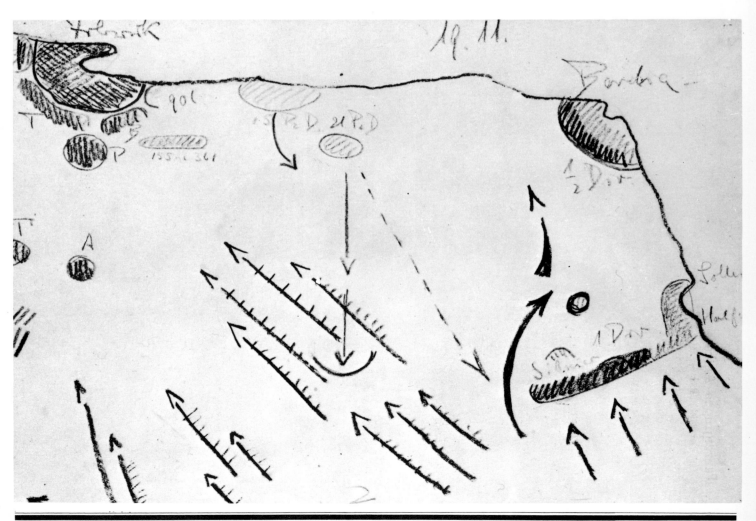

part of the armored formations and there were in addition several hundred more in reserve. This was well above the number possessed by the Axis who had about 400 with no reserve, though in numbers of men the two sides were about equal. It had been the accretion of these forces which had delayed Auchinleck's attack, but he claimed it was necessary as he had to counteract the advantage his opponents had with shorter supply routes.

The British offensive was code named Crusader, and began on 18 November with one British corps taking up positions masking the Halfaya Pass, while the other pressed forward across the desert in three columns of which the central one was to make for Tobruk whose troops were to break out at the appropriate moment. This part of the attack went well and came within 10 miles of the port, taking the airfield of Sidi Rezegh. On its left flank, however, the 22nd Armored Brigade ran into stiff opposition from the Italian Ariete Division and on the right the 21st Panzer Division (the old 5th Light) held the advance of the 4th Armored Brigade.

Although he was at first taken by surprise, by the second day Rommel had realized exactly what was intended and sent two armored divisions to Sidi Rezegh to try to prevent a link-up with

Below: An American-built Stuart tank of 7th Armored Division (the Desert Rat emblem can be seen on the tank's right track-guard).

the Tobruk garrison. This had already begun its breakout, but had to abandon it when the relief force meeting it was held. The extremely confused struggle lasted until 22 November, though by the afternoon of the 19th it was clear that the point of the British spearhead had been blunted. Nonetheless, largely thanks to the efforts of General Freyberg's New Zealand Division, Tobruk was actually relieved to the accompaniment of wild celebration in London.

The battle became more confused than ever. Rommel conceived a scheme to force the British into withdrawal by swinging his own forces southward and toward the Egyptian frontier where their sudden appearance was bound to be unnerving. This was certainly true. Cunningham, who had been considering abandonment of the entire offensive, now became even more worried, but was prevented from issuing the relevant orders when he was peremptorily replaced by Ritchie on the orders of Auchinleck, though Churchill wanted the Commander in Chief, Middle East to take personal control.

All the same the German and Italian forces had to pay for their own daring. The speed with which Rommel demanded that the movements be made led to an inextricable disorganization. This was brought home to Rommel when he and General Crüwell, commanding the Afrika Korps, got lost and finally broke down behind British lines in Rommel's Mam-

Above: General de Stephanie commanded the Italian Ariete Division which fought well during Crusader in the Sidi Rezegh area.

moth. With Indian dispatch riders and other troops round them, they struggled to get their vehicle started and were finally able to make off.

This was not his only such intimate contact with the enemy. On 23 November, again driving his Mammoth, he came upon a field hospital. The battle was at that time in a highly fluid state and field hospitals were hard to move because of the wounded. From its position Rommel could only surmise it was a German one and he was actually walking the wards, accompanied by a British doctor (who said afterward he took his visitor for a Polish officer), before he realized his error and foreshortened his visit somewhat abruptly. There were, as it happened, a number of German wounded present who had watched goggle-eyed as their commander in chief passed their beds. Mercifully they all had the presence of mind not to draw attention to him.

As far as the battle went Rommel's next effort was to try to cut through the British line and reestablish the siege of Tobruk, but this came to nothing. The Italian Ariete Division failed to arrive and the commander of the 15th Panzer Division received a fatal wound. Fuel and ammunition were running low, besides which it was gradually becoming

clear that the first optimistic German estimates of British losses and their effect upon the offensive were wildly optimistic. Blunted it may have been; it was not yet over.

Though Rommel did not know it and probably never discovered, fate had actually played an almost unbelievable trick on him. His own forces, desperately short of supplies of every kind, and advancing southeast toward the Egyptian frontier in the hope that victory there might give them access to enemy supplies, had driven past two enormous British dumps. These, several square miles in extent, lay near Gabr Saleh and were being guarded by purely token forces which DAK could easily have swept aside. One of the German units actually touched the edge of a dump without realizing its existence thanks to the skill used in camouflaging it.

In the first week of December, Rommel was forced to abandon all hope of retaking Tobruk, knowing that its garrison could further strengthen the British forces. To add to his miseries on Christmas Day, Benghazi fell. The British offensive had advanced 300 miles. In letters to Lucie, whose despondent tone is all too clear, he blamed the failures on the Italians and the exhaustion of his own troops. The first charge is extremely unjust, however, for the Italians had fought with great determination and spirit and, as their commanders pointed out, they too were capable of feeling exhaustion. Save for the fortresses of Bardia, Halfaya and Sollum, the Battle for Cyrenaica had ended.

When Bardia, Halfaya and Sollum finally fell, 4000 German and 10,000 Italian prisoners were taken. Battle losses up to that time had been about equally matched at around 18,000, but this completely altered the proportion. British tank losses were certainly higher than Auchinleck would have liked, but on the other hand it was now he who was master of the field and could send out the recovery trucks to bring back any tanks which could be repaired. However, the British had hoped for a quick, decisive campaign. Churchill had even talked of another Waterloo or Blenheim. Thanks to Rommel's skillful handling of the retreat they had got neither. Both sides had fought themselves to a standstill and despite their casualties, the Axis armies were still in being, while, on Auchinleck's estimate, it would be mid-

Below: German Messerschmitt Bf 109 E fighters over the desert. They are from the First Staffel of Jagdgeschwader 27.

Right: Rommel's sketch of a possible
attack on 29 December 1941. In fact he did
not advance until 20 January 1942.

February before he would be in a
position to resume the offensive.

For Rommel, 1942 began badly with
his forces back at El Agheila. Of all his
huge losses, the most critical were in
tanks, for he had just over a couple of
dozen of his original 412 left. He had
also lost 800 of his 1000 aircraft and the
British had gained an air superiority
they were never again completely to lose
and which would add immeasurably to
the miseries of the Axis forces. As always
Rommel claimed to be astonished at the
unwillingness of the British to pursue
with vigor and attributed this to the
caution of their generals, overlooking the
fact that, like him, they could suffer
supply difficulties, particularly as lines
became stretched by advances in an area
where there were few roads and no railroads. However, in the conviction that
he was to be granted a period undis-
turbed, Rommel was already planning
fresh offensive action of his own, which
is, in itself, a tribute to his enormous
resilience.

On 5 January a convoy carrying 55
tanks and 20 armored cars as well as
antitank guns arrived at Tripoli. Rommel
seized the opportunity these gave him
and on 20 January launched his first
counter-stroke which began as little more
than reconnaissance in strength. A tank
column with Rommel himself in the
lead encountered the British 1st Armored Division which had recently relieved the veteran 7th. New to desert
fighting, they were decisively beaten,
losing 100 of their 150 tanks.

To some extent these British reverses
were because of a new development in
the war – the entry of Japan and the need
for Britain to try to defend her Far
Eastern possession which led to transfers
from North Africa to Malaysia and
Australia. It was also due to the fact that
by their own advances the British had
vastly extended their supply lines once
more and were suffering from all kinds
of shortages, details of which German
radio-interceptors picked up. Blame
must also attach to Ritchie and Auchin-

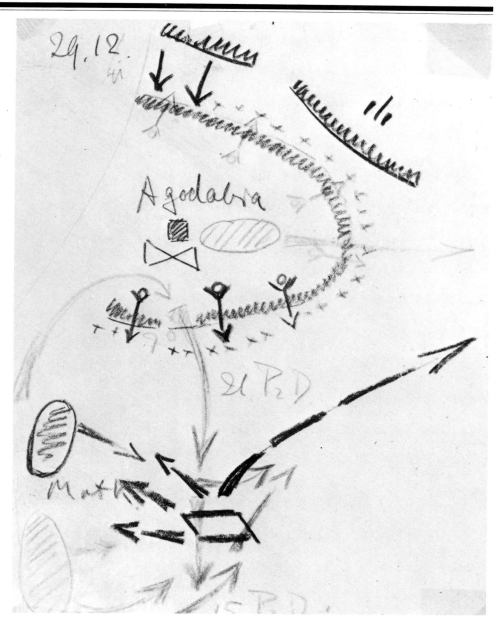

Right: Rommel's sketch of a possible
attack on 29 December 1941. In fact he did
not advance until 20 January 1942.

Right: A German Mk III tank is landed at
Tripoli. The availability of reinforcements
was a vital factor in all desert battles.

leck who miscalculated their enemy's ability to recover and had failed to act with sufficient speed and boldness themselves. Indeed, they had no further offensive plans until mid-May.

Despite protests from the Italians who believed Rommel was gambling at much too high odds, Rommel continued to press the enemy. His own confidence had been strengthened by a demonstration of Hitler's own esteem for him. He had been given the Swords to his Knight's Cross with Oak Leaves. Although Commando Supremo threatened to reduce supplies to Rommel because of his unwillingness to modify his ambitious plans, on 26 January he still decided to make for Benghazi. Always a lucky general, he was blessed once more: his column ran into a sandstorm which though it made their going unpleasant also concealed it. Sealed first on its north side, then on the south before the defenders awoke to what was happening, Benghazi fortress fell on the 29th pro-

Below: General Bastico and other Italian officers pass an abandoned British fuel dump in Benghazi in early February 1942.

viding so much booty it was possible to equip many units of the Panzerarmee from it. Rommel now thrust east recovering much of Cyrenaica and forcing the British back to positions based on the triangle Gazala-Bir Hacheim-Tobruk.

Coming on top of the victories of the Japanese forces in the Far East, this was an appalling blow to morale in Britain. Churchill found it necessary to go to the House of Commons to seek a vote of confidence and in the course of his speech paid a generous and characteristically chivalrous tribute to Rommel. 'We have,' he said, 'a very daring and skillful opponent against us, and, may I say, across the havoc of war, a great general.' It was not only in Britain that there was anxiety. In New Zealand and, especially, in Australia, which might itself shortly be facing a Japanese onslaught, there was the greatest alarm and, in many quarters, a demand that their forces in North Africa should be brought back to be used for home defense purposes.

Rommel was to write that it was his experience that bold decisions 'give the best promise of success,' though he is careful to differentiate between strategic

and tactical boldness and sheer gambling – where defeat could lead to the total destruction of the general's own forces. His boldness had succeeded, perhaps in many ways beyond his own expectations. With his three German divisions (he always omits the Italians), the British had been kept fully stretched and repeatedly beaten. If the British premier felt compelled to offer praise to the enemy commander, this was only a small voice amid the fanfares of appreciation for his achievements now coming from his own country. Here he was, once more, the hero of the hour. Radio programs were interrupted to bring the news of the recapture of Benghazi. The mention of his name in a speech by Hitler brought a long and noisy ovation. An overjoyed Lucie was the recipient of an endless stream of telephone calls, cards, bouquets. There were further honors and decorations. In Berlin Rommel's old friend, Josef Goebbels, was giving him the usual star treatment, using his successes as a means of making the contrast with failures elsewhere. As the propaganda minister's German biographer, Viktor Reimann says, he completely

Below: A Junkers 52 transport aircraft in flight over the North African coast. The Ju 52 was the most widely used German transport. It could carry up to 18 fully armed troops.

Bottom: Men of the Afrika Korps at a machine-gun post in the desert. They use a tripod-mounted MG 34. This weapon could also be used as a bipod-mounted squad light machine gun.

Below: Reinforcements for the Afrika Korps arrive by Ju 52. The picture was almost certainly taken in 1941 because sun helmets were only issued in the early stages.

Left: A German propaganda picture of a desert patrol soon after Rommel arrived in Africa. The sandy ground is not typical of the North African battlefields but where it occurred it was a real check to mobility.

Far left: A Messerschmitt Bf 110 twin-engined fighter. Although it could not stand up to combat with the best Allied single-engined fighters its longer range and heavy armament served it well in the Mediterranean.

Below left: The crewmen of a German Kubelwagen scout car watch as a dust cloud blows toward them across an airstrip. Aircraft used in North Africa were fitted with special air filters to protect their engines from dust.

Below: The original caption of this propaganda picture was 'Knights of our Times.' It shows a German Mk IV tank with a short-barrelled 75mm gun. Rommel's forces used them in France and North Africa.

Far left: A German motorcycle combination in the desert. The machine gun could be detached and used in a normal infantry-support role.

Left: An RAF armorer works on the fuse of a 250-pound bomb on an airfield 'somewhere in Egypt.'

Far left below: RAF groundcrew work on a Beaufighter. Versions of the Beaufighter were used as long-range fighters and as torpedo bombers.

Bottom: The aircraft carrier *Santee* during the Torch Operation late in 1942. By this time the Allies had air superiority throughout the Mediterranean.

Below: A German gun in action during the siege of Tobruk. Rommel did not have enough artillery to break into the defenses.

Left: Prisoners taken from a British Commando unit during the fighting in Tunisia.

Below: A B-17 Flying Fortress on a North African airfield. Hitler rushed troops to North Africa after the Torch landings to try to prevent the Allies taking forward bases for such bombers. Rommel got little of this help.

Right: German troops inspect the wreck of an American P-38 Lightning downed near Tunis.

Below: American troops pass an abandoned German Tiger tank early in the Italian campaign. Tigers were also used by the Germans in the Kasserine battle.

Bottom: American paratroops prepare for an operation. The yellow ring around the white star was introduced as a special identification mark for Operation Torch.

Below: Sherman tanks were first used by the Allies at Alamein. It became the principal American and British medium tank for the rest of the war.

overlooked that in other theaters generals were obliged to put a brake on Hitler's audacious and often ludicrous schemes. In the desert, Rommel was free to do as he pleased.

The North African commander was shown on newsreels and constantly mentioned in radio bulletins. Photographs of him in his now familiar cap and British goggles appeared in magazines and newspapers almost daily. Sacks of fan-fail brought him, in his own words 'piles of letters from all manner of females,' many it seemed anxious to displace the fortunate Lucie. Although the writers were usually young, among them was one unknown lady who simply signed herself 'The Old Hag' and whose admiration for general and troops was boundless, although she often betrayed a strain of anti-Nazism and openly expressed her detestation of Nazi propaganda. This seems merely to have amused Rommel who, on one occasion, when she sent a parcel of books which were found to be of the variety banned in the New Germany, had them distributed to the troops.

He was, as already mentioned, by no means averse to publicity. At his headquarters he always had a huge bag of postcard portraits taken by Hitler's official photographer, Hoffmann of Munich, and this was kept replenished with supplies sent out from Germany. Every letterwriter was rewarded with one of these, personally autographed by the great man. Many are still treasured. The unpleasant Hanke, attached to his staff during the Battle of France, had

been succeeded in North Africa by a Lieutenant Alfred Berndt, a great burly figure who reminded other staff members of a bear. Like Hanke, he tried to give the impression that he wielded great power in Berlin. He also seems to have been totally unscrupulous, once boasting how he had dressed in Czech army uniform at the time of the Munich crisis to organize 'provocations' which were made to appear as if carried out by the Czechoslovaks themselves. He noticed, among other things, that Rommel enjoyed being filmed or photographed and would automatically fall into a dramatic pose when he knew the cameras were on him. Since the various attempts on his

Above: Four Italian officers with Iron Crosses. Rommel thought little of Italians generally but always rewarded individual bravery.

life, which had shown how greatly he was feared by his opponents, Rommel was able to say that he encouraged self-publicity for reasons of morale.

By the beginning of February, it was clear that the British had escaped and that the Axis lacked the means to intercept them. Once more the battle lines became static as both sides planned fresh

Below: A German slit-trench during one of the static periods of the North African campaign when both sides were assembling supplies.

Above: Passing the time during the lull in the fighting in the spring of 1942. Soldiers of both sides had few entertainment facilities.

efforts. The entire desert campaign tended to take on this stop-go character and both Rommel and his British counterparts complained that their superiors seemed unable to understand why it was they could not constantly be on the offensive. This was inherent in the nature of a struggle being fought by armies at the end of extremely long supply lines. Thus, one side or the other would amass men and material and launch an offensive, hoping this would break its enemy before its own resources had been used up. In practice this climax was never achieved. On the British side, generals were under political pressure to attack before they had acquired the overwhelming superiority they believed necessary to final victory. On the German side, supply was in Rommel's view both inadequate and tardy, though this was not always true and he never considered the needs of other theaters.

However, the lulls in the battle were hardly vacations for the troops involved or their commanders. In the main they were all-too-short breaks in which every effort had to bent towards preparation of defense and the organizing of the means for delivering the next blow. They did, on the other hand, give some opportunity for relaxation, though, as his associates commented, Rommel took

little advantage of them. Once or twice, finding himself by the seaside, he and his party would strip off for a quick swim. His only other recreation, though he rarely indulged even in this one, was his old favorite, the chase. One of his aides, Heinz Werner Schmidt, recalls how he was a member of a party which made a foray into the country south of

Below: Rommel, already beginning to look tired and drawn, is seen outside his barely furnished desert tent.

Gazala in search of gazelle. It was, he says, organized with the precision of a military operation, carefully drawn up plans being prepared for the interception and slaughter of whatever game came their way. He goes on to describe how a herd of gazelle was pursued across the desert by men in fast-moving military vehicles, driven, as he says, 'in a suicidal manner,' until at last one wretched animal had been separated from its companions and repeatedly overhauled by the cars as their occupants took shots at it. Rommel finally brought it down.

On the whole, however, Rommel made heavy demands on his subordinates and did not spare himself. This is consistent with the philosophy he tried to impart in his days as director of Wiener Neustadt military academy where he told graduates at passing-out parades that they must be an example to their men in both their duty and private life; they must never spare themselves and let their troops see that they did not. In a characteristic touch of psychological insight he also urged them, besides being tactful and well mannered, to 'avoid sharpness or harshness of voice, which usually indicates a man who has shortcomings of his own to hide.'

Over the weeks from February, Rommel's forces were being reinforced though, by his standards, all too slowly, and Commando Supremo in Rome seemed not at all to view his successes

with the same rapture they had created in Germany, even going so far as to take some Italian troops from him. He himself flew back to Germany to gain Hitler's direct support and was still there at the end of the month, spending some of the time with his wife and son.

In the British War Cabinet there was apprehension all through the spring lest the Germans attempt an amphibious assault on Malta, keystone of the Mediterranean strategy, and this led Churchill yet again to harry Auchinleck to return to the offensive. Auchinleck insisted he would act only when his armor and supply positions permitted.

Cabinet fears were all too well founded. After a meeting between Hitler and Mussolini it was agreed that such a landing should be attempted, but only after Rommel had first taken Tobruk. Plans for these attacks had been laid as early as mid-April and outlined to the Italians. The first blow would be a feint

at the northern end of the British line near the coast. This would be delivered in such strength as would compel the British to transfer their armor from the inland end of the line to meet it. Adequate time would be given for the British to do this before the real attack began with an outflanking movement round the south. At the same time to prevent another retreat behind the Tobruk perimeter, flying columns would be pushed ahead to seize the port. All the praise seems to have turned Rommel's head and he was never more cocksure, boasting of the speedy seizure of the immediate objectives and of further dazzling victories thereafter. Once more he had Cairo and Suez back in his sights.

The assault began on schedule at 1400 hours on 26 May 1942, and the first stages seemed to justify Rommel's confidence. To add conviction to the feint, a Panzer battalion and a unit equipped with captured enemy tanks was attached

to the forces delivering it. These were withdrawn at dusk to reinforce the main assault which was being made by some 10,000 vehicles. Despite the fact that the first blow did not come entirely as a surprise, the British still reacted as Rommel had hoped and took the feint seriously. The outflanking move therefore began under the conditions planned for it, though again it did not come as the surprise Rommel intended. German intelligence had failed in two important ways, however. First, it had not discovered the arrival on the battle scene of the new American tank, the Grant. Secondly, it had not appreciated how strong and well-organized the British defenses were.

One of the Italian units, the Trieste Division, part of XX Corps protecting the German left flank, missed its road and

Below: The early stages of the battle on the Gazala Line. The British forces were poorly led in this battle.

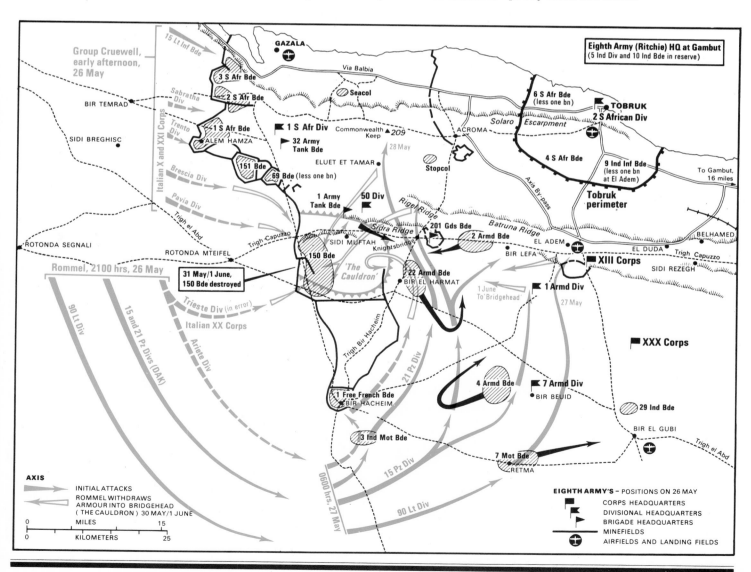

stumbled into a defensive box, held by the 150th Brigade, covering the main road junction. The inferior Italian tanks were given an extremely rough handling.

The 150th Brigade box also brought disaster of another kind. For some weeks, the DAK commander, Crüwell had been laid low with jaundice, but had recovered enough to take control for the offensive. His Fiesler Storch was shot at while flying over the box and forced to land and he was himself taken prisoner. At one point he was even mistaken for Rommel, either because of the similarity in their names or because both flew Storchs. The story of 'Rommel's capture' got as far as Moscow, leading to a fresh spate of photographs appearing in the German press to show he was still with his troops. For a time, he hoped to mount a rescue operation, but when this proved impractical appointed General Walther Nehring, lately arrived from the Eastern Front, to command the Afrika Korps.

The crisis of the Trieste Division was not the only one to beset the Italian XX Corps. Its other division, Ariete, detailed to attack the Free French forces

holding Bir Hacheim, found they had met their match and were held. Despite this setback the German DAK spearhead continued its wheel round and behind the British.

For carrying on his plan regardless of what was happening elsewhere, Rommel deserves the fullest praise. But fate was against him on this occasion. The strongly held 150th Brigade box was like an uncharted rock to an attacking armada and was situated across the intended supply lines for the German forces. It therefore had to be eliminated. This had to be done at a time when the panzers were already running short of fuel and the supply convoys had failed to arrive. In addition, the losses among both Germans and Italians had been unexpectedly severe.

This was plainly a check to Rommel's plans. He had also failed in another respect. The promise of quick and easy victory might impart an initial dash to an attack, but troop morale is liable to undergo a drastic change if units run into unexpected and determined opposition. They then feel misled and confidence in

Above: Lieutenant General Nehring took command of DAK when General Crüwell was taken prisoner late in May 1942. Below: A German Mk III tank drives past the vehicles of an infantry unit. The tank carries a long-barrelled 50mm gun – an effective weapon.

Right: Ju 87 Stuka dive bombers return from a mission. After mid-1942 the Allies had air superiority throughout North Africa.

command plummets. Exactly this happened to Rommel's forces and in some places elite German units turned tail and fled the field, while a spate of rumor further increased disintegration.

A British attack at this moment would have had the most devastating effect. The Panzerarmee would have found themselves pushed into the minefields and in this position surrounded. It could well have been the end of the Axis in North Africa. In contrast with the sometimes overimpetuous Rommel, the British Eighth Army commander, Ritchie, held back, no doubt partly because he had in mind Auchinleck's planned offensive and did not want to dissipate forces being husbanded for it. Even when Rommel threw his main strength against the 150th Brigade box no counterattack in strength was made, though this would have revealed Rommel's weakness. As a consequence, its courageous defenders were themselves forced back,

finally surrendering on 1 June after supplies had been exhausted and they had been relentlessly bombed by Stukas, although the indomitable Free French continued to hold out at Bir Hacheim after this.

As the pressure on the 150th Brigade grew, Auchinleck urged Ritchie to attack to relieve it and continued to do so after its surrender, realizing the serious situation which had now developed and being in particular mindful of the posi-

Above: British troops surrender in front of
a Grant tank. The picture was taken on 16
June 1942 shortly before Tobruk fell.

tion of the French garrison. When
Ritchie did attack, on the night of 1–2
June, it was far too late. Rommel had
taken advantage of the time allowed him
by a dilatory enemy to reorganize. It
foundered against well-placed German
guns.

Another effort on the 5th was equally
ill-fated and such British units as managed to pierce the German defenses
round what had come to be called The
Cauldron were pushed back in a well-
timed counterattack.

After a struggle in which at first little
had seemed to go in his favor, Rommel
had broken through the Gazala Line. All
that remained, isolated but still holding
out, was the Bir Hacheim garrison at its
southernmost end and a enclave held by
troops of XIII Corps in the north. The
Panzerarmee was in a position to strike
where its commander wished and to
strike fast. It was therefore to Bir

Hacheim that he now turned his main force. Such attempts as were possible were made by Eighth Army and particularly by the RAF to harass the enemy and drop supplies from the air. On 10 June, however, General Koenig was authorized to break out, which he did successfully, rejoining the main British force with 27,000 men. They had fought for 14 days, in a defensive battle which has often been compared with the epic of Verdun 26 years earlier. This citadel of the Gazala Line reduced, Rommel next decided to break out The Cauldron and to destroy the British XXX Corps opposing him.

At the other end of the line withdrawal of the surrounded XIII Corps was carried out by the troops slipping through the sector of the line held by the Italians to its west, then making a wide detour well to the south of Bir Hacheim to reach the main Eighth Army lines. Risky as this was, since much of the corps' transport was on its last legs, it was safely accomplished by 96 percent of the corps.

Tobruk was now back in the front line

Below: German forces move into Tobruk on 21 June. Moving away from the camera is a captured British 'Quad' artillery tractor.

Above: Tobruk after its capture. The Germans gained vital stocks of fuel and food when the fortress fell.

and its future was as worrying to Westminster as it was to the generals on the spot. Auchinleck ordered that the port be held and the enemy be prevented from besieging it, a strategy which in fact was the reverse of what the military circumstances dictated. A more realistic view was that the British should withdraw their entire Eighth Army to the line of the Egyptian frontier, giving themselves the opportunity for regrouping and reinforcement.

However it was ruled that XIII Corps should hold the port and its immediate environs. The XXX Corps, now severely diminished, would provide a kind of mobile force, partly to harass an approaching enemy, partly to strengthen the frontier defenses but a series of attacks upon its depleted forces compelled the abandonment of those points from which it could fulfill its first role. The Battle for Tobruk would have to be fought by XIII Corps alone. It braced itself for the task, Ritchie's plan now being to allow a temporary investment of the fortress until it could be rescued by the coming British offensive. The commander on whom the responsibility fell, the South African General Klopper, was lacking in relevant experience and no coordinated plan had been drawn up, though Tobruk was well garrisoned and adequately, even lavishly, provisioned. By the 18th, the Axis forces stood solidly round its perimeter. Meanwhile XXX Corps was withdrawn to the frontier with the intention that it should assist by sending out flying

columns to menace the advance.

On 20 June the Panzerarmee struck at first light. In his earlier attempt to take the port, Rommel had been handicapped by lack of plans of its defenses. Not only had this been rectified, but in addition he had studied the successful British attack of 1941 and taken note of the fact that it had been directed at the southeast corner. He, therefore, decided to approach in the same direction. The attack took the by now traditional *Blitzkrieg* form with a screaming Stuka assault followed by a breakthrough of massed armor. The defense was dogged but hopeless and XXX Corps's attempts at diversion did not deceive the Germans sufficiently to distract them from their main intent. By midmorning, there was a one-and-a-half-mile deep gash in the defensive line; by 1600 hours the airfield had been taken. As it became obvious that the port area itself could not be held, a feverish attempt was made to deny its facilities to the enemy by demolition. This was forestalled by the timely arrival of a fast-moving mobile force.

Another defensive perimeter was organized with promises by Klopper that he would fight to the last man and the last round. It soon became clear that such a task was a useless waste of human life. On the morning of the 21st, Klopper asked for terms. Tobruk had fallen and

Above: Tobruk harbor. On hearing of this German success Roosevelt immediately ordered extra shipments of Sherman tanks to be sent to Africa.

30,000 Allied troops marched into captivity. Total British losses through the offensive had been about 50,000, compared with the Germans' 3360, though officer-casualties had been disproportionately high.

Booty from Tobruk included enough fuel for a hundred miles of further advance and, to the delight of the troops, a wide variety of luxuries, among them bread, tobacco, foodstuffs and beer from Munich which the British quartermasters had bought in Lisbon.

If he had been popular after the fall of Benghazi, Rommel was now a hero to the German people. At home, Lucie heard the radio announcer ask listeners to stand by for a special news bulletin and thought it would be to declare that Sebastopol had been taken by Manstein's troops. Amazed and delighted, she heard instead the news of Tobruk's fall after only 24 hours' fighting.

Hitler announced the immediate conferment of a field marshal's baton. At 49 he was the youngest of that rank in the German army. Even his Italian detractors either fell silent or else changed their opinions overnight. British morale, on the other hand, fell to what was perhaps its lowest point in the entire war, not excepting the period after the Fall of France.

Churchill found himself faced by a fresh and more ominous political crisis than that of the preceding January. A member of his own Conservative Party had put down a Motion of Censure for debate and this would have meant the dismissal of the government if it had succeeded in gaining a majority. During

Left: Some of the many British prisoners after the fall of Tobruk. Successful attacks in the desert always took many captives.

Above: The newly promoted Field Marshal Rommel scouts a British position. He clearly looks tired and unwell.

the debate, Rommel's name was mentioned several times. The prominent socialist, Aneurin Bevan, declared that had he been so ill advised as to join the British army he would have remained a sergeant because of his social background. (This was, of course, exaggeration. Rommel came of precisely the same sector of society as many British commanders.) Churchill himself used the German general's skill as an excuse for failure. In fact, the censure vote failed by 475 votes to 25, but it was hardly to be expected that the enemy propaganda machine would miss the opportunity handed it by the British House of Commons. Hitler, in personal conversation, even went so far as to attribute much of Rommel's reputation to the praise heaped upon him by his adversaries – conduct which he found quite incomprehensible.

In retrospect much of the anxiety felt in Britain at the time seems unnecessary

and arose from a basic misunderstanding of the nature of armored war in the desert. Rommel had once likened it to a battle at sea where whoever had the longer reach and the greater mobility possessed the advantage. He was, of course, perfectly right, as the British commanders had gradually learned, but had failed to convince their masters in London. As in a sea battle, the action shifted over wide areas. Victory was not to be counted in the seizure of terrain, it would be final only when the enemy's vessels had been driven to port and kept there by a superior enemy patrolling the roadsteads.

This seems to have been perfectly clear in Auchinleck's mind when, on 16 June, he wrote to the British prime

Below: A German armored car. Both sides made extensive use of armored cars throughout the desert war. This vehicle carries a 20mm gun.

minister telling him that Tobruk would be defended even if 'temporarily isolated' by the enemy. Churchill claims he understood this to mean that the fortress was to be held at all costs even if the Panzerarmee by-passed it, to form, as it had previously, a threat to the German communications. It is plain, however, that Auchinleck, assessing the situation in purely military terms, saw things differently and was quite prepared for it to fall. In this he lost sight of moral realities. Tobruk, because of its epic defense under siege earlier, had come to stand as the very symbol of the British will to resist. Its fall made it appear as if this will was itself weakening.

Once Tobruk had been taken the Axis leaders dithered. The Luftwaffe reconnaissance spoke of the remnants of the Eighth Army withdrawing toward the Egyptian frontier, bemused, disorganized and exhausted. An immediate attack might have converted this into rout. However Commando Supremo's authorization for the attack on the Gazala Line was conditional on Rommel advancing only to the wire of the Egyptian frontier.

Besides the Italian High Command, there was another tier in Rome. This was represented by Field Marshal Albert Kesselring, a Luftwaffe officer, who held the title of Commander in Chief, South. He made repeated visits to Rommel's headquarters and, on the 21st, the day of Tobruk's fall, flew there yet again with the purpose of curbing the Panzerarmee's impetuosity. The most important thing at this juncture, he insisted, was Malta, whose capture as planned

Below: A German half-track artillery tractor, towing an 88mm gun, pauses during the advance after the fall of Tobruk.

would remove the threat to Mediterranean supply routes. There is little sign that Rommel was in the mood to heed. The booty from Tobruk gave him the potential for further advance and he meant to use it.

Rommel was undoubtedly right, for not to have done so would have been to

Right: Rommel and Field Marshal Kesselring. Before becoming Commander in Chief, South, Kesselring led Luftflotte 2.

exchange the substance of achievable victories immediately for the shadow of the capture of Malta. The British had now come to realize the high price their own tardiness in evacuating the Gazala Line had extorted. With the enemy so close on their heels, they would lack the breathing space needed to convert the Egyptian frontier into a tenable defense line. To reform their tattered units they would have to pull back farther still. Ritchie, therefore, roughly split his forces, basing them on Mersa Matruh on the coast road and Sidi Hamza inland. Between them lay a belt of minefields and it was Ritchie's intention to take Rommel in flank if he attempted to sweep round southward. Auchinleck, having visited the front, was doubtful whether Eighth Army was in any condition for such ventures and on 22 June sent Ritchie on leave and himself took command of his forces.

His first decision was to order that instead of a stand at Mersa Matruh or Hamza, the defenders would roll with the punch, retreating as far as was necessary to avoid a head on contest they were unlikely to win. To slow down an advance by Panzerarmee a line of brigade boxes was created between the two points.

In the meantime in Berlin and Rome

Below left: German and Italian soldiers plunder a British supply dump in July 1942. British rations were of better quality.

Below: Tires quickly wore out on stony North African ground. Those shown here were part of the booty taken at Tobruk.

Left: German troops enter Mersa Matruh on 28 June 1942. The advance continued but supply problems were acute.

Tobruk and included a wide sweep round the city to cut the eastern coast road behind and thus sever the escape route. By the time the British had realized what was happening, the panzers were streaming from the frontier in three columns, two south of Mersa Matruh and one south of Hamza. A check to the most southerly advance near Bir Khalda did not stop the other two columns from reaching the coast road. Auchinleck was perfectly clear how to respond, but the execution of his orders suffered from confusion and signals delays so that relief movements either did not take place at all or took place only when it was too late to affect the issue. On 28 June Mersa Matruh was in German hands.

Now the Germans were well inside Egypt. Gunfire could be heard in both Cairo and Alexandria and panic was seizing these two cities. The only obstacle which stood between them and the enemy was the position around the small railroad station at El Alamein.

a change of heart seemed to have occurred. Suddenly, both were aware of the prizes awaiting them in Egypt. The Malta invasion was postponed and it was decided to use bombing to contain the island. Rommel was free to cross into Egypt, though it seems certain he would have done so anyway.

He was perfectly well aware that the British were withdrawing on Mersa Matruh and on 26 June began to attack it. This was very much like the attack on

6:CHECK AT ALAMEIN

In Africa Rommel was exultant once more. His letter written to Lucie on 30 June telling her of the fall of Mersa Matruh crowed, 'We are already 60 miles to the east. Less than 100 miles to Alexandria.' Tired as they were from the struggle, these feelings of exultation were shared by the Panzerarmee, its Italian no less than its German units, and they showed no hesitation in pursuing the enemy and seeking to prevent his escape. In fact, at the time Rommel was writing, they were at Fuka through which the British had passed only a few hours before them and where some were caught. Both sides knew that El Alamein would be the next point of resistance, though the Axis troops and their commanders seemed to have convinced themselves it would require little effort to subdue. Mussolini had even flown to Cyrenaica ready for his triumphal entry into the Egyptian capital.

The Panzerarmee's strength was desperately depleted, but Rommel was banking on the belief that the British

Left: Weary infantry of the Afrika Korps continue the advance toward Alamein. The soldiers carry entrenching equipment.
Below: A German 20mm antiaircraft gun. It could fire 220 rounds per minute and hit aircraft at 6000 feet.

were still weaker, badly demoralized and disorganized as well. He was very nearly right. Auchinleck had only two battleworthy divisions plus the equivalent of a division of armor, though this was not yet organized as a cohesive unit. On the other hand, there were certain ominous signs which should have served as a warning to Rommel. Among these was a massive increase in British air activity which forced him to move his own headquarters several times to reduce losses. Several members of his staff, including his batman, had been injured. As well as this Auchinleck was clearly getting at least some supplies and possibly reinforcement. In fact at that moment he was awaiting the arrival of the desert-experienced 9th Australian Division from Syria.

The terrain in which the next phase of the battle would take place was very different from that further west in Cyrenaica where, on a battlefield of more or less infinite dimension, each side could theoretically outflank the other continuously. About 40 miles to the south of El Alamein lay the Qattara Depression which, by every test, was impassable by armor. Nonetheless, there were insufficient British troops to man a continuous line between El Alamein and the Depression, and after disposing the 3rd South African

and was not able to disengage until a sandstorm blew up at noon. The troops then recommenced their encircling movement, but were soon in fresh trouble from the guns and mortars along the defensive perimeter. Normally cool and intrepid, they showed symptoms of panic, some units even making for the rear. It required all the persuasion of their officers to get them back to the battle front. Rommel, who intervened in person, had a taste of the British artillery when one shell exploded only six feet from his car.

Initially the Afrika Korps fared somewhat better. One of its divisions ran into the British defenders at Deir el Shein. The other came to its assistance and after fuelling and scouting they again attacked at noon and penetrated the British perimeter in the area.

Despite the setbacks elsewhere, Rommel believed the Afrika Korps had prised open the gateway to Alexandria as he had convinced himself that the defenses, 'the Alamein Line,' as he called it, consisted of a continuous belt. Subsequent events at first seemed to confirm this analysis. At 1800 hours all resistance at Deir el Shein ceased and that

Above: A German engineer lifts a British-laid mine. Real and dummy minefields were used extensively by both sides to bolster defensive positions, especially near Alamein.
Right: Rommel's forces had few of this version of the Mk IV tank with long 75mm gun at Alam Halfa or Alamein. Its fighting power was comparable to the Sherman's.

Brigade in an arc round El Alamein, where they stood guard over road and railway, Auchinleck placed the remainder of his forces in small groups. These were unlike the brigade boxes favored by Ritchie in that it was intended that they should be highly mobile and mutually supportive where his had been fixed.

Rommel's own plan was precisely the same as that he had used against so many of the coastal towns: a sweeping movement round to the south, then a lunge, with one column cutting the coastal, escape road, while another assaulted Alamein itself. The first part would be undertaken by the Afrika Korps with the Italian XX and X Corps in support; the second, by the 90th Light Division. At 0300 hours 90th Light moved off, ran head on into the defenses of El Alamein

night radio programs in Germany were once more interrupted to announce the breaching of the Alamein Line. However, no optimism could conceal the cost. The Afrika Korps had sacrificed 18 tanks. Worse still, time had been lost and this had allowed Auchinleck to position his 1st Armored Division with 119 tanks, 38 of them the new American Grants, behind Deir el Shein on the Ruweisat Ridge.

Rommel, for his part, was focussing attention on the area of the El Alamein perimeter and the region to the southeast. He realized it was too strongly defended to be entrusted to the 90th Light unaided, and directed the Afrika Korps to turn northeast and so assist in the drive to the coast road. This was actually playing into Auchinleck's hands for he was planning an outflanking movement by forces in the southern sector of his front, the spearheads advancing westward and so into the Panzerarmee's rear. When the Afrika Korps tried to advance along the Ruweisat Ridge it was repelled and by nightfall the British could feel confident that for the time being the German attacks had been halted.

This was indeed the case, though

Above: A knocked-out British Valentine tank left behind during the German advance. The Valentine was reliable but poorly armed.

Rommel intended to make one further effort the next day, using the combined forces of the Afrika Korps and the 90th Light to drive to the coast, while employing the Italian Trieste and Ariete Division to contain the British forces on his left or southern side. The Afrika Korps' moves were checked by the British 1st Armored and the Ariete Division ran into continual resistance as it advanced against New Zealand troops. By noon on 3 July it had lost almost all its tanks and had only two guns left.

A shocked Rommel urged the Afrika Korps to a renewed, final effort. It made limited progress then stuck. The Panzerarmee was strung out over a line 35 miles long and forced to dig in lest it was attacked. Worse still there was a gap in the line caused by the failure of the Italians to reach their objectives and little with which it could be plugged.

Fortunately for Rommel, the British with a rare chance of bringing him to his knees, were dogged by the belief that the Axis forces were much stronger than they actually were, and acted with unnecessary and costly overcaution. They responded nonetheless and Rommel was compelled to withdraw westward although by evening he realized that there was little sign of hot pursuit. The 90th Light and the Afrika Korps's 15th

Panzer Division were in a pitiful state and needed relief while they were refitted. The only way he could grant them this was employing the Italian XXI Corps. This in itself represented the measure of his desperation, since hitherto Italian units had never been put into front line positions where their possible defection could be calamitous.

It was to prove an appalling error. Auchinleck no sooner realized what was happening than he saw it was the weak point in the Axis defense and struck at

Below: A German infantryman begins to dig in. Rommel's German infantry units were usually very much understrength.

it. On 11 July the 9th Australian Division and the 1st South African Division advanced westward out of the Alamein perimeter, making for Tell el Eisa. In the subsequent struggle the Italian Sabratha Division was almost entirely destroyed, while the Trieste Division on its right suffered almost as badly. However, if the Germans were inclined to blame the debacle on their ally's unreliability they had scarcely done better themselves. A raid on a position held by the 15th Panzer Division to the west of Ruweisat Ridge was taken for a full-scale attack and a panic call for assistance sent out.

Auchinleck, to give maximum strength to the northern thrust, had moved his XIII Corps from the area just north of the Qattara Depression, gambling that the gap so created would go unnoticed as, at first, it was. When it was spotted, it was thought that only one division had been moved and not the entire corps. Just the same Rommel believed that here was a weakness for exploitation and detached 90th Light to take advantage of

it, its strength being augmented by the Italian Littorio Division. Apparently under the delusion they were about to run into a fully manned defensive line, the attackers squandered a massive bombardment on an empty sector – a second uncharacteristic error.

However, Rommel's optimism had re-established itself and he was again thinking of Alexandria. He was awakened both from these hopes and from sleep by the attack on the Italians at Tell el Eisa. His own headquarters was only three miles from the town and for the moment holding off the enemy until an escape had been effected was the only preoccupation of his staff.

On hearing the news of the collapse of the Sabratha Division, Rommel saw at once the threat a further British advance could pose to his line of supply. He cancelled the attacks in the Qattara region and rushed as many troops as possible back north. He was now being forced on the defensive with the initiative passing to the British.

Three days later, on 14–15 July, there were further attacks and the Italian X Corps in the Ruweisat Ridge area suffered devastating losses. Renewed at-

tempts by Auchinleck's forces to advance westwards on 21–22 July progressed slowly, but helped to keep up pressure on the Axis. However, it was plain the momentum was going from British attacks, while the defenders' line was stabilizing behind the broad belts of minefields. Temporarily, the crisis was over, but the hoped-for easy victories had eluded the Panzerarmee and its commander. On the 20th, a bitterly disappointed Mussolini returned to Rome. He looked, according to an eyewitness, 'desperately ill and tired.'

It is, of course, not this first battle of El Alamein, fought under the banner of General Claude Auchinleck which has gained and held the world's attention. It is the second one, fought under General Bernard Montgomery which is best known. Yet it was the first battle which was the more crucial. It saved Egypt and the Canal. However it even went a step further than this. For the first time since Rommel had come to North Africa, a British commander could say he had his measure. If the Germans attacked, Auchinleck declared in late July, they would strike for the southern end of the British front sweeping round

Below: An Australian manned 6-pounder antitank gun at full recoil after firing. The 6-pounder superseded the 2-pounder.

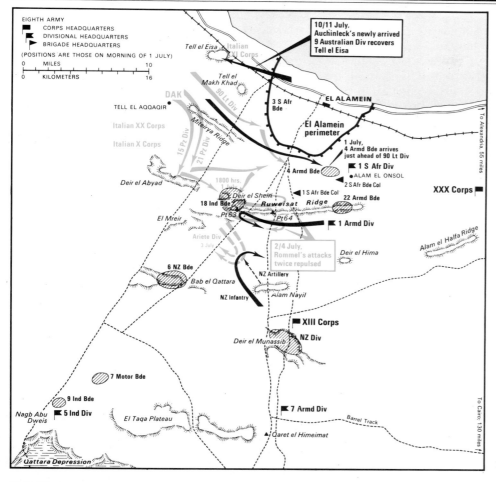

EIGHTH ARMY
CORPS HEADQUARTERS
DIVISIONAL HEADQUARTERS
BRIGADE HEADQUARTERS
(POSITIONS ARE THOSE ON MORNING OF 1 JULY)

| 0 MILES | 10 |
| 0 KILOMETERS | 16 |

10/11 July,
Auchinleck's newly arrived
9 Australian Div recovers
Tell el Eisa

Tell el Eisa Italian XI Corps
Tell el Makh Khad

EL ALAMEIN

DAK
TELL EL AQQAQIR

Italian XX Corps
Italian X Corps

90 Lt Div
Miteirya Ridge
15 Pz Div
21 Pz Div

3 S Afr Bde

El Alamein perimeter

1 July,
4 Armd Bde arrives
just ahead of 90 Lt Div

1 S Afr Div
ALAM EL ONSOL
2 S Afr Bde Col

XXX Corps

Deir el Abyad

1800 hrs, 1 July

Deir el Shein

18 Ind Bde
Pt63

Ruweisat Ridge
Pt64

1 S Afr Bde Col   22 Armd Bde

1 Armd Div

El Mreir

Ariete Div
3 Jul

2/4 July,
Rommel's attacks
twice repulsed

Deir el Hima

Alam el Halfa Ridge

6 NZ Bde
Bab el Qattara

NZ Artillery

NZ Infantry   Alam Nayil

XIII Corps
NZ Div

Deir el Munassib

7 Motor Bde

9 Ind Bde
5 Ind Div
Nagb Abu Dweis

El Taqa Plateau

7 Armd Div

Barrel Track

Qaret el Himeimat

Qattara Depression

To Alexandria, 55 miles

To Cairo, 130 miles

Left: This German armored car is unarmed and instead carries the distinctive framework of radio aerials of a command vehicle.

Left: Although Rommel attacked again in September the first battle of El Alamein shown here was a decisive setback.

to try to reach what they would take for the rear in the Alam Halfa area. Defensive preparation had been made for just such a contingency and any German initiative along these lines would be brought to a bloody halt. The confidence with which Auchinleck could express himself was indicative of the changed situation in the North African campaign brought about by the First Battle of Alamein.

However, Churchill and the British War Cabinet were not interested in how German attacks were going to be stopped. They only wanted to know when the Eighth Army itself was going over on to the attack to achieve the final victory over the Axis forces which had been allowed to tarry too long in the Middle East. Auchinleck promised it would come in late September. For Churchill and some of his colleagues it was too long to wait. This was not just natural impatience at work; there were strategic considerations as well. The German summer offensive in Russia was pushing toward the Caucasus. If the worst came to the worst and they broke through, the backdoor to the oilfields would be open. This made the Panzerarmee's defeat even more vital in Churchill's view as Eighth Army might have to defend Persia. Besides, he was involved in negotiations with the Americans over the form of their participation in the war and it would be easier to get his own way if he had a British victory to present to them.

Auchinleck had, of course, a double role. Appointed as Commander in Chief, Middle East, he had also been commander of the Eighth Army since he dismissed Ritchie, and although there was some question of simply finding a replacement Eighth Army leader, it was finally decided to make two new appointments.

In early August Churchill was in Cairo and soon after his arrival another British general, Sir Harold Alexander, arrived there. Although already earmarked for a post with the Anglo-American forces then being organized,

Above: Major General Kleemann, the commander of 90th Light Division, pictured talking to one of his aides on 13 July 1942.

it was decided to give him that of Commander in Chief, Middle East. There remained the question of the Eighth Army command and Churchill himself favored General W H E Gott, nicknamed 'Strafer Gott' on account of his ferocity, who was already holding command in North Africa. However, while flying to Cairo on 7 August, his plane was shot down and he was killed. There was only one other person available, General Bernard Montgomery – an officer who, by chance, had already fought Rommel in France, having taken part in the Battle of Arras in which the 7th Panzer Division had fared so badly.

On 15 August the supercession took place and Auchinleck departed, in the eyes of many disgraced. It was left to Rommel himself to redeem his reputation for him. He was, the German said, a good leader, a man of personal courage and deliberate action who had succeeded in what he set out to do, namely to prevent a German advance into Egypt. It was, nevertheless, a backhanded compliment to Rommel that he had caused so many changes in command among his enemies during his time in North Africa.

Auchinleck's conduct of First Alamein had had a further effect. From that time can be dated the breakdown and slow disintegration of the Panzerarmee and the failure of its commander's health. Pictures of Rommel taken at the time show him pale, tired and drawn. Sheer physical causes had much to do with this: he had been in the desert longer than most men and certainly more

Right: Major General von Vaerst and Lt Colonel Westphal at the same meeting as Kleemann above. Rommel was fortunate in his subordinates.

than men of his own age. Nonetheless one senses that a victory at Alamein would have given him a new lease on life.

From about 2 August it had become obvious to those around him that Rommel was a very sick man. His stomach and liver were at the root of the trouble and one of Germany's leading specialists in these fields was flown to North Africa. He wanted Rommel to go home for proper treatment. This was dismissed as impossible for the time being as he had plans for another breakthrough attempt and, until its completion, treatment on the spot had to be organized.

As part of this a proper kitchen was installed at his headquarters and a good cook found, while his diet was augmented by supplies of fresh fruit and vegetables and by the produce of the hunts with which his brother officers filled their spare time. Hitherto, Rommel had been subsisting on the same rations as those supplied to the men and one of his aides told Lucie, in a letter explaining her husband's condition, that he was not told he was receiving extras lest he refuse them. This is a little hard to credit. He can hardly have supposed his troops were enjoying such luxuries, particularly when the diseases of malnutrition were rife among them.

For his part Rommel was blaming his misfortunes on the battlefield on the old scapegoats – the feckless Italians and the

failure to supply him, in which both they and the German liaison officers in Rome were to blame. There was some substance to these strictures, but also a great lack of understanding. The Italians were doing their utmost; their seamen braving the British blockade to cross the straits. Reinforcements were arriving at the rate of 1000 men a day. The total of around 13,000 new troops which reached him included the first two regiments of a new division, the 164th Light, and the crack 1st Paratroop Brigade, under its commander, General Hermann Ramcke, which had fought with distinction in Crete, as well as an elite Italian unit, also with a distinguished history, the Folgore Parachute Division.

These increments were what Rommel proposed to use in his new offensive. Large-scale diversionary attacks would be launched against the northern and central sectors of the British line while the main assault, by the 90th Light, the Afrika Korps and the Italian Ariete and Littorio Divisions would fall on the southern sector between Bab el Qattara and the Depression itself. There was even talk of an advance across the Depression, but it was rejected on the grounds that the sand was too soft and

Left: An Axis transport unloads in a North African port. In the late summer of 1942 many of Rommel's supplies failed to arrive.

the enterprise too risky when the Panzer-armee was so short of fuel.

The battle took precisely the form Auchinleck had forecast. On his arrival, Alexander had accepted his predecessor's defense plan which was to hold 'as strongly as possible the area between the sea and Ruweisat Ridge and to threaten from flank any enemy advance south of the ridge from a strongly defended position on the Alam Halfa Ridge.'

In contrast with the sick Rommel, determined nonetheless to see the battle through before returning to Germany for treatment, the Eighth Army was now under the command of the sprightly Montgomery. The similarities between the two men have often been pointed out and certainly existed. Both came from much the same sort of background in their respective countries. Both were men who lived frugal, even austere, personal lives. Both were energetic and thrusting with a large degree of self-

conceit and with that conviction of their own rightness, often invaluable to a leader, but infuriating to others. Thereafter it is differences rather than similarities which are striking. Montgomery had none of his German opposite number's intuitive flair, his *Fingerspitzengefühl*, 'the feeling in the fingertips' which enabled him to take risks and frequently to get away with them. The British commander was a supremely cautious man who struck only when he knew everything was in his favor and thereby sacrificed opportunities Rommel would have used to advantage.

In achieving his ideal conditions Montgomery was also much luckier than his predecessors at Eighth Army headquarters who had had to fight with what they had. Every possible effort was being made to supply and strengthen him, and the Americans had joined the struggle by this time. In particular British air superiority was fully estab-

Below: Heavily laden German infantry move up to the front late in July 1942. Despite reinforcements Rommel's infantry remained weak.

Above: General Montgomery gives orders to a group of officers. General Horrocks, commander of XIII Corps, is to Montgomery's right.

lished, making the lives of Panzerarmee's troops extremely unpleasant, though in the organization of the tight cooperation between ground and air forces in the coming weeks, Montgomery's own part has to be fully acknowledged.

Rommel did not expect a British initiative before the end of the month and was proved right. Montgomery, not to be hurried into an ill-prepared offensive by anyone, was gathering his resources for a major thrust in the El Alamein region. It was therefore the Germans who struck first on the night of 30/31 August.

Soon after passing through their own minefields, the attackers found themselves in an unsuspected British one. That the area was much more heavily defended than German intelligence estimates had made out was also shown by the heavy bombardment which fell round the ears of the hapless Afrika Korps as they struggled through the mines. This was soon accompanied and succeeded by bombing attacks from the RAF who, of course, knew just where the enemy was to be found. (The Germans never discovered that the radio codes they believed foolproof had been cracked.)

Despite the hammering it had received which had seriously upset the attack schedule – Rommel's plan called for a 30-mile advance by night and nothing near this had been achieved – the Afrika Korps was still prepared to go on. The plan was slightly modified, however, and instead of a broad sweep eastward, the turn was to be made in the region of Alam Halfa Ridge. After re-

fuelling and reconnaissance, the move began at 1300 hours on 31 August. A sandstorm blew up and impeded progress, while the Italian units were late in arriving and remained permanently behind the Germans instead of protecting their flank. Then the tanks ran into soft sand which made the going heavy and depleted their limited fuel stock. When nightfall and the sandstorm cleared, the RAF came out of the blue to recommence its assaults using parachute flares to light up the entire area and thereby stopping all movement.

One division of the Afrika Korps continued to advance on 1 September, then ran out of fuel, while by daylight the air attacks continued. Rommel records that between 1000 and 1200 hours that morning they were bombed no fewer than six times. He himself had to take cover in a slit trench and saw a spade lying beside it pierced through with a bomb fragment. At the same time, the British artillery was pouring down shells at an estimated rate of 10 for every single

Below: A British 5.5-inch gun during a night action. Montgomery planned an extensive bombardment before the Alamein attack.

Right: The Battle of El Alamein. Rommel constructed an elaborate system of defensive minefields all along the line between the coast and the impassable Qattara Depression. However, he had to split his armor into two groups because he did not have enough fuel for a counterattack from a central position.

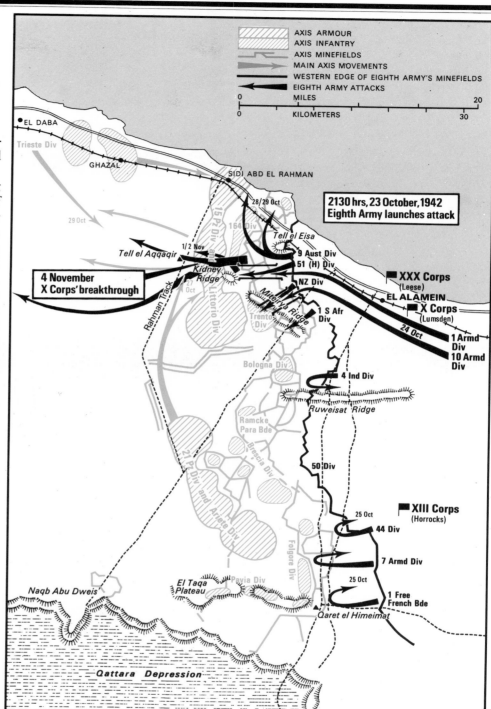

German one. By evening the Panzer-armee had only one day's issue of fuel left.

Air attack was equally unremitting and next day Rommel decided to call off his offensive on the night of 2 September and retire toward Bab el Qattara. This was done with little harassment from the British armor which Rommel ascribed to Montgomery's cautious approach, though Montgomery himself claims he had in mind a strong counterthrust but that the main reason it was not executed was because he did not want Rommel to withdraw beyond reach as an 'army in being.' All the same, attacks were mounted by the New Zealand Division, though they were called off on the night of 3/4 September.

In analyzing the battle Rommel attributes his own failure to three factors: the strength of the British position in the south; the heavy, nonstop air attacks to which his forces were subjected which impeded and often prevented all movement; and the shortage of fuel. Not only history but his contemporaries have been less kind to him. Among critical observers of his conduct of the battle was Kesselring, the Commander in Chief, South, who pointed out that, since Afrika Korps's move on Alam Halfa had already turned the British flank, all they had to do was to press their attack with determination to break through. As to the shortage of fuel, he suggests that existing supplies could as easily have been employed in advancing, which would probably have brought them to British dumps, as in withdrawing. The reality of the matter is, of course, that Rommel did just precisely what his opponents expected of him and they were ready for his moves.

Whatever the merits or demerits of the case, it had undoubtedly been costly. Panzerarmee casualties numbered nearly 2500 and they had lost almost 600 prisoners. They had also lost 50 tanks, 15 field guns and 35 antitank guns. British losses were 1640 men killed, wounded and missing. Eighteen antitank

guns were lost, and while the British tank losses at 68 were obviously high, the British were now in a position to afford this.

With the battle over, Rommel was free to go to Germany for treatment of his liver condition, but it was not until 18 September that his replacement arrived. He was General Georg Stumme, big, placid and an expert in tank warfare. In the interregnum, the troops were employed in strengthening the defense of the El Alamein sector and this task was continued under Stumme's command.

On 23 September Rommel left for Germany, his departure being monitored by the British listening posts. On the way he paid a courtesy visit to Mussolini who decided, probably rightly, that his illness was largely psychological, the result of the disasters he had suffered.

For a few days he stayed with Goebbels and his family. Hitler, surprisingly in the circumstances, was thinking of Rommel as Commander in Chief of the entire German army and Goebbels seemed anxious to push this proposal. On 30 September he was actually seen

produced to undertake so mammoth a task, but of the material promised only derisory amounts ever reached the front. On 3 October after a press conference in which he could not restrain himself from the promise of future African triumphs, Rommel flew to the mountain resort of Semmering to begin his cure and was met there by Lucie.

Thus it was that he was absent when

Below: The Allied forces in the Middle East were from many nationalities. These attacking infantry are Czechoslovakian.

Above: Rommel waves to the crowds at the Sportpalast rally on 30 September 1942. Field Marshal Keitel is beside him.

by Hitler at the Reich Chancellery and, very belatedly, handed his field marshal's baton. It was then agreed that he was to hold his present position until the Panzerarmee had been rested and reinforced. That evening he was guest of honor at a Nazi Party rally held at the Berlin Sportpalast, venue of so many National Socialist gatherings carefully orchestrated by Goebbels.

He felt able to tell Stumme in a letter following his meeting with Hitler that equipment soon to be sent to him would include the new giant Tiger tanks, the 250 mm mortar and the Nebelwerfer multiple rocket-launcher. These were to be conveyed in a new kind of ferry developed by the German engineer, Siebel, which was of such shallow draft that torpedoes simply passed under it. As Rommel was later to discover, not only was an insufficient number of these

Below: A mixed battle-group of Sherman tanks and infantry vehicles rehearses an attack before El Alamein.

Right and below right: Typical pictures of the German positions before El Alamein. Mines barbed wire, slit trenches and antitank ditches were established all along the line.

Montgomery's great offensive at El Alamein began on 23 October. In the circumstances of the struggle, the British commander's caution is to some extent understandable. As Rommel himself had found, the line from the coast to Bab el Qattara was not capable of being turned and could only be broken by frontal assault, always costly. Montgomery's plan was to drive two corridors through

the enemy mine fields due west of the Alamein station through which armor and infantry could deploy. Diversionary attacks would be mounted along the rest of the front.

For this purpose Montgomery had mustered 11 divisions of which three were armored, and these were all organized into three corps. Rommel himself had 13 divisions but only four were German and these were well below establishment. The 15th Panzer Division, for example, had something approaching a third of its normal strength because of sickness. In all there were only 29,000 combat-fit troops out of a total of 46,000, while Rommel's force of 550 tanks, of which 320 were Italian, was confronted with 1029 British, including 500 American-made Shermans. This substantial buildup had taken time, and it is a strange reflection that Auchinleck had lost his job because he could offer no offensive before late September when Montgomery's did not take place until late October, nearly a month later.

The attack opened with an extremely heavy artillery barrage. The infantry assaults then began and the corridors were opened, but could not be made wide enough for uncongested movement. German counteraction was hesitant, however, one reason being Stumme's death from a heart attack while his car was being strafed by British aircraft on the 24th. Luckily on 20 September one

Below: Italian artillery during the Alamein battle. The artillery was the most effective arm of the Italian army.

of the German General Staff's foremost armor experts, General Wilhelm von Thoma, had arrived in Africa and he was able to take over. Nonetheless, for several crucial hours the Panzerarmee was leaderless.

On 24 October Rommel was told of the attack by telephone from Berlin and that Stumme was missing (his body was not recovered for several days). He was asked if he would be willing to return and said he would. A few hours later Hitler himself was on the line and repeated this inquiry, but told him not to take off until he had heard further, as it would be unnecessary to interrupt his

Below: All Rommel's infantry suffered heavily during the Alamein fighting. This picture was taken on 7 November 1942.

cure should the British offensive show signs of flagging. A second call came at midnight, and on 25 October Rommel found himself once more in Rome and was told of the seriousness of the German situation at Alamein and also of the increasing difficulties in supply because of sinkings by the Royal Navy.

It was dusk when he reached his headquarters. The story he heard did nothing to lighten an already gloomy mood. Casualties had been high and as well as this there was such a shortage of fuel that only local counterattacks could be made. There were difficulties with spare parts so that only 31 out of 119 German tanks were serviceable and the British superiority in shell was such they could often fire off 500 to every single German round. Besides all this, the defenders

Above: Oberst Fritz Bayerlein was Chief of Staff to Rommel in 1942 and replaced von Thoma in command of DAK in November.

were suffering the remorseless attacks of the RAF. To increase their problems Alexander's air-force commander, Air Marshal Sir Arthur Tedder, had ordered a massive raid on Tobruk Harbor during which yet another tanker was sunk.

However, the British were not finding things going entirely their way and there was even talk of calling off the offensive. The attackers were still penned in a restricted area with further mine fields in front of them. After Rommel's return,

known to the Eighth Army through their radio intercepts, the German resistance also showed greater cohesion. However, Montgomery knew that his own reputation, no less than the fate of Egypt and perhaps the whole war, was at stake and he was therefore determined to go on. In some parts of the front units were regrouped; in others, the lines of attack were shifted and then shifted again whenever resistance showed no sign of breaking. Between 30 October and 2 November this determination paid dividends, though at first unnoticed by the attackers.

At 2015 hours on 2 November Rommel and Thoma jointly decided to withdraw to positions to the west, round Fuka. Late the following night the 4th Indian and 51st Divisions began breaking through. That day Rommel received a message from Hitler himself, the first of many to follow in all theaters of war. There would be no retreat. The Panzerarmee would hold its positions until 'victory or death.' Rommel, devoted to his Führer, was thrown into conflict. He was anxious to obey, but 'this crazy order' had come 'like a bombshell.' For 24 hours he struggled to conform, only to find it 'demanded the impossible.'

Thus were born his first fearful doubts about Hitler's leadership. These would follow a vacillating course, but the general trend was for them to increase. In this case even the short postponement of the withdrawal had had serious consequences. By 4 November the British 1st, 7th and 10th Armored Divisions were through and Panzerarmee had no option

other than still further retreat. Not even a visit by Kesselring in which he tried to persuade Rommel to accept the 'no retreat' order could change this and the meeting resulted only in a bitter quarrel between the two men.

This infamous order had quite a different effect on Thoma. For a short time he became commander of the DAK when Nehring was summoned to other duties. On 4 November he put on all his medals and after denouncing the order as 'sheer lunacy' drove off in his tank to the center of the battle then raging. He was there taken prisoner by the British and that night was Montgomery's guest at dinner. At Rommel's headquarters there were many who believed that he had intentionally surrendered himself to the enemy. His place at the head of the Afrika Korps was taken by Fritz Bayerlein, former Chief of Staff to Rommel.

The British seemed not to have realized the extent of their victory and the losses they had inflicted on the Germans. Panzerarmee casualties totalled something near 36,000, of which 13,000 were German. In numbers the Afrika Korps was down to a regiment, the 90th Light Division had about one and half battalions and the 164th Light had lost about two-thirds of its stength. Worst of all they were left with only 12 tanks.

As to the retreat, this began as a pell-mell withdrawal under British air bombardment but in the end was turned into something more orderly and succeeded in achieving its objectives. The Panzerarmee commander knew he had at least kept his forces in existence.

7: ROMMEL IN RETREAT

A strong belief in Rommel's near infallibility had spread beyond the limited confines of the battlefield to the neutral powers. To this conviction, the defeat at El Alamein came as a considerable blow. Only a few weeks earlier at his press conference in Berlin, he had told reporters, among them neutral correspondents in the capital, that there would be no retreat. 'What we have we hold,' he had declared. It began to appear that the tide had turned.

By 5 November Panzerarmee safely reached Fuka where some preparations for defense had been carried out by the Italians who arrived there first. It helped too that the old post-victory lethargy against which Clausewitz warns had seized the British and they lacked enthusiasm for the chase, but largely because of the failure of the Italian units the line was easily penetrated once it was reached. The defenders, compelled once more to withdraw, found themselves prey to the RAF. In the end, Fuka was almost as great a victory as Alamein.

Left: An American 105mm gun in action near Kasserine. Lavish US resources turned the tide in this battle.
Below: These German troops have managed to hold on to their captured British trucks and guns.

Then, during the afternoon of the 6th, Rommel's luck turned and a rainstorm began, heralding the start of the wet season which that year began early. The change this wrought in the landscape was spectacular. Sandy desert became quagmire. The wadis, those dry, natural chasms which crisscrossed the arid terrain, became what they really were – watercourses. There were never enough bridges. For the troops on both sides it made life even harder, but tactically it affected attackers more than defenders. The Axis forces were retreating along the coastal roads; the Allies, whose only hope was to outflank, needed firm, dry terrain for their armor. The rain gave Rommel 24 hours' respite and by 7 November a stop line had been established round Mersa Matruh but on the 8th there was a new and, from the German point of view, most alarming development.

Immediately upon America's entry into the war in late 1941 and following upon Roosevelt's decision that the European enemies must be defeated before Japan, the question had arisen of where the first blow was to fall. The American Chiefs of Staff favored landings in mainland France; the British believed unless this was done in overwhelming strength and with meticulous preparation it would

making a dash for Tunisia some 400 miles away. By the first days of November, the Germans had got wind of imminent landings, but believed they would be directly behind Panzerarmee. On the 7th, Rommel was warned to prepare coastal defenses.

The landings actually took place on the 8th against relatively slight opposition from French colonial troops. In the next few days the Eastern Task Force, made up of American and British units, hurried east along the coast and by the 12th was at Bône near the Tunisian border which was crossed four days later. However, the Germans had responded with a speed which seems to have taken everyone by surprise. Troops and equipment were shuttled across the Mediterranean by air until an entire army, the Fifth Panzer Army under Colonel General Jürgen von Arnim, a veteran from Russia, was squeezed into Tunisia.

This achievement was watched by Rommel with deepening bitterness. 'What we found really astonishing,' he wrote, 'was to see the amount of material that they were suddenly able to send to Tunisia, quantities out of all proportion to anything that we had received in the past.'

All this time Rommel's own Panzerarmee was still in retreat. A plan to stand

end in disaster. What the British proposed instead was a plan for landings in North Africa in the rear of Panzerarmee. Feasibility studies tended to support the British view as far as European landings were concerned, but there remained a notable lack of eagerness among the Americans for the North African project

Below: Allied forces come ashore at Oran, 8 November 1942. Steel matting has been laid on the beach to prevent trucks getting stuck.

until the threat of Rommel's advance toward the Suez Canal, whereupon it was revived.

At the same time, it was felt that the British proposal for an invasion of Tunisia would be too risky as the sea journey would bring the attackers into close proximity to strong Axis naval and air forces. The compromise reached was for landings at three places along the Moroccan and Algerian coasts with the forces landed furthest east, at Algiers,

at Halfaya Pass came to nothing after news of the landings reached him. The pressing need was to shorten the supply lines and consolidate his own and Arnim's forces. He therefore decided to pull back as far as El Agheila. On 9 November Sidi Barrani was evacuated, on the 13th Tobruk and on the 20th Benghazi. It was now clear that Eighth Army's advance was not going to trap Panzerarmee, and Montgomery spent the final days of November and the be-

ginning of December in regrouping and reorganizing his own supply lines.

The El Agheila position was to be defended in Rommel's scheme by a double chain of delaying outposts, one near Agedabia, the other near Mersa Brega scene of earlier, more fortunate encounters. The decision marked an important stage in a violent argument in which Rommel was pitted against the Italians, against OKH and finally against Hitler and the party leadership itself. He

Above: British infantry rest outside Tobruk before moving in to reoccupy the town. Rommel's retreat continued.

had long been trying to persuade his masters in Rome to come to see the situation for themselves. On 24 November they did, Kesselring being accompanied by Cavallero from Commando Supremo, as well as by Bastico, now once more Rommel's nominal superior. The meeting quickly degenerated into a

Above: A soldier of 51st (Highland) Division rests during the advance. Rommel's 7th Panzers captured most of the division at St Valéry but it was rebuilt to fight in Africa.

quarrel when the visitors insisted that Mersa Brega, which Rommel had seen only as delaying point in his retreat, should be held at all costs. He forthwith presented them with a shopping list of his needs to achieve this, but recognized that they neither understood nor really wanted to understand the realities of the situation. This was confirmed after the trio returned to Rome and sent Rommel fresh orders to hold Mersa Brega with the added stipulation that Commando Supremo itself would have to give the order for withdrawal from it.

Infuriated by these directives, Rommel decided to fly to Germany and try to win Hitler's support. Their meeting took place on the afternoon of 28 November at 'The Wolf's Lair,' the Führer's advanced headquarters at Rastenburg in East Prussia, and from the outset Rommel was aware of a coolness toward him. He had hardly begun to outline his case when Hitler launched into a tirade in which he accused the Panzerarmee of every military crime down to cowardice in throwing away their weapons in retreat. All through this the bold warriors surrounding Hitler stood nodding their heads like porcelain mandarins. Once

more Rommel was told to hold on to the Mersa Brega line.

He left Rastenburg not only lacking the support he needed but placed under the additional handicap of having the Reichsmarschall, Hermann Goering, sent back with him. On the journey to Italy it soon became obvious that Goering had ambitions of his own in North Africa. He ordered his personal janissaries, the 'Hermann Goering' Panzer Division of the Luftwaffe to be sent there. All that Rommel could gain was Goering's support for a withdrawal farther west because he was persuaded that this would enable the German forces, including his own division, to

strike against the Anglo-Americans in Tunisia; victory, particularly against the Americans, would obviously redound to his greater glory.

On 12 December the British attacked the outpost line at Mersa Brega and, ordered by Rommel to show flexibility rather than engage in a major battle, the local commander withdrew on the 13th. Again the British followed with their usual timidity. They had not yet gotten rid of the fear that Rommel might spring a surprising and terrible riposte – the easier the victory the greater their fear. Early on the 14th German air reconnaissance observed a British outflanking move coming round the south of El Agheila and the town had to be evacuated, too. An attempt to win time was made by sending out a mobile force against the British 7th Armored Division east of El Agheila and while it succeeded in this aim, the cost to Panzerarmee in lost tanks was considerable. A further battle, consisting largely of isolated struggles, took place on 15/16 December, but again Rommel's forces managed to escape a planned trap and withdrew from the Agheila region altogether.

In the meantime the Allied advance in Tunisia was encountering increasingly strong opposition for rain was also making movement difficult there. On Christmas Eve 1942 the commander of the Anglo-American forces, General Dwight Eisenhower, was forced to acknowledge that the race to Tunisia had

Below: German parachute troops in Tunisia. During Rommel's African campaigns German paratroops were used strictly as infantry.

Above: General Anderson (left) commanded First Army in the Kasserine battle. General Bradley led US II Corps.

been lost. The Axis bridgehead there, quite easily supplied from Italy, had on one side mountain ranges through which the attacking troops would have to break, and on the other a line of fortresses built by the French before the war, the Mareth Line.

It was toward this that Rommel was trying to hurry his men. Physically ill and deeply depressed, there is no doubt that Rommel was viewing events through the darkest possible glasses. A quite open 'defeatism' had been remarked on in many quarters during Rommel's visit to Rastenburg in November and it is likely that it was only his reputation which prevented action from being taken against

him on that account. Undoubtedly he exaggerated his own difficulties and though this must have been an attempt to persuade those above him to increase their support, and perhaps also to give him an excuse for later failures, it seems certain that he really believed things to be almost as bad as he claimed. On the Italian side, Marshal Cavallero remarked on the blackness of his mood and Kesselring agreed. Rommel still had 'quite a good hand of cards, if only he would play them,' he said. Even the British were astonished by the unremitting flow of complaint from Panzerarmee headquarters which their intercepts picked up. He seemed to be in a state of paranoid fear.

Whatever the causes, one can only pity him. His days seemed to have been passed in a miasma of deepest gloom. His

sole relief, he said at the time, was travelling out to see the men at the front and he was especially delighted to come across anyone from his own region, Swabia. He had always tended to hark back to his days at Wiener Neustadt, which he had often declared were the happiest period of his and his wife's life. At this time he did so more than ever. On Christmas Eve, driving back from a visit to an outpost, he and his group ran into a herd of gazelle and shot one down. But that night he wrote home, 'My worries are as big as ever.'

Desmond Young believes that this was the time of Rommel's final disillusionment with Hitler, whom he saw as perfectly willing to sacrifice the lives of men in useless stands to keep him in power a little longer. There is something to this belief, but more important, in Rommel's calculations, was the entry of the United States into the war, particularly in North Africa. He appears to have believed that this was due to Hitler's own hasty declaration of war on the United States the moment Japan began hostilities and to have failed to realize Roosevelt was only waiting for the moment when he could win his people over to participation in the struggle.

David Irving appears to assume that illness – Rommel was still subject to sore throats, headaches, giddiness and bouts

Below: Rommel with Marshal Cavallero (center) and General Bastico (right). Their authority over Rommel was nominal.

that Rommel, devoted husband and father, would have considered a course which would have had such unpredictable effects on those he loved.

However, the state of his mental and physical health was to have a significant bearing on events to come. When one contemplates him at this period one can only be left with admiration for his remarkable stamina and fortitude, and with astonishment that his collapse was not more complete. To add to his problems there were the complexities of the command structure so that every decision he made had first to be referred to the Italian Commando Supremo in Rome for approval. Inevitably there was procrastination which could last for days and

Above: A German officer takes a quick meal during the fighting in Tunisia. Rommel's supply position was little improved by retreat.
Right: An Me 323 transport aircraft in Tunisia. These giant aircraft had a vast carrying capacity but were dreadfully vulnerable if attacked.

of fainting – combined with defeat were temporarily disturbing Rommel's capacity for lucid thought. He even goes so far as to suggest Rommel was considering the prospect of final defeat and capitulation and, in his utter disillusionment, perhaps saw them as offering relief to his suffering. There had been precedents of course. Paulus, with whom Rommel had been a captain at Stuttgart in his early career, and who had visited North Africa on behalf of the General Staff in the first months of Rommel's command there, had capitulated at Stalingrad and then thrown in his lot with the enemy to the extent of joining a group of dissident German officer prisoners who were doing propaganda broadcasts for the Russians. Nearer home, there was Thoma, his own DAK commander. As evidence, Irving adduces a secret letter sent to Lucie on 21 December in which Rommel asks, 'Haven't you sent off that English dictionary to me yet?' If Rommel was of a mind to surrender himself and his troops, he must certainly have lost all mental stability. When Thoma defected, special efforts were made by his former brother officers to prevent the fact from becoming known in Berlin because of the reprisals likely to be visited on his family. It is, therefore, hardly credible often came at the crisis of the battle. Usually orders, when finally received, would be quite contrary to Rommel's intentions and take no account of the realities of the battle on the ground. He must also have been aware that his health was giving an excuse to those who wanted him gone.

On 16 January Montgomery caught up with and attacked Panzerarmee at Buerat. The 15 tanks of 15th Panzer Division faced 100 British machines, but in skillfully laid traps 20 of these were destroyed, while the 90th Light Division threw back an attack by the 51st (Highland) Division which had penetrated an outpost line.

Rommel at first believed that this was

no more than a holding attack whose purpose was to prevent a retreat while the main Allied strength was brought up but plans found on a captured British officer showed that the objective was Zauia, 30 miles west of Tripoli along the coastal road. This meant that the real intention was to encircle Panzerarmee. At other times he would certainly have felt capable of responding positively to such a situation of which, after all, he had prior notice. He had now so persuaded himself that the only way in which he could save his army was by constant retreat that on the 19th he ordered his forces to pull out of Tripolitania altogether. Tripoli, which had eluded Wavell, therefore fell to Mont-

Below: Once Rommel's forces retired to Mareth there was some leisure for the men.

gomery who thus gained a magnificent harbor at a moment when he was in such difficulties with his communications that he was on the verge of abandoning the offensive.

The Italians who had seen first one gem of their colonial empire, Cyrenaica, lost and then this second one, now began to add their voices to those begging for Rommel's replacement. On 26 January he was told by Commando Supremo that he would be 'released' from his command as soon as he reached the Mareth Line so that he be able to have the medical treatment he needed. An Italian army command was to be formed under General Giovanni Messe who arrived in Africa shortly afterward and this would incorporate the German units. However, Rommel decided to stay until he received a formal dismissal from Germany.

Mareth had by this time been reached and over the next few days Rommel was occupied with examining its defenses and bringing them up to an adequate state to meet an assault from Eighth Army. In particular he was concerned that this line, like the Maginot Line in France itself, was incomplete and could be outflanked. However he reached Mareth with time in hand and soon became convinced that the British would not attack so formidable an obstacle until they were well prepared. Therefore, sick as he was, he began contemplating offensive action.

The most serious result of the loss of the race for Tunisia was, as far as the Allies were concerned, the fact that they had no ports within easy reach of their front. The nearest harbors were those along the Algerian and Moroccan coasts which left a long haul overland to the front. For a time Eisenhower toyed with the idea of driving southeast across Tunisia to Sfax, but was persuaded by the British that before attempting anything of this sort he should wait for Montgomery to reach Marath when the forces there would be tied down.

Tunisia is bisected by two mountain ranges: the Western and Eastern Dorsales and the Allied line ran roughly down the Eastern Dorsale with its coastal terminus about 40 miles to the west of Bizerta. Unwilling to remain idle, Eisenhower decided to extend his line southward, employing for the purpose the American II Corps, which was to concentrate in the area of Tebéssa. The effect of this deployment in the south was, however, to extend the corps thinly along a line 100 miles long behind which there were few routes allowing a rapid consolidation in any threatened area. This did not go unnoticed by Rommel.

In attacks in January von Arnim's Fifth Panzer Army in Tunisia had retaken two of the passes in the Eastern Dorsale which had been held by a courageous but ill-equipped and unmechanized French unit. This unit was now being pushed backward toward the Western Dorsale. The possibilities opened up were not lost on Rommel. He suggested to von Arnim that their two armies should be used in combination. Fifth Army would advance eastward and Rommel's forces northward through the US II Corps sector with the two forces breaking out of the passes in the Eastern Dorsale round the area of Kasserine.

Once this had been achieved the way lay open, through the enemy rear, to Bône and Constantine. The Allied armies would be surrounded and the struggle in Tunisia could well be at an end. The Axis forces could then turn in unison on Eighth Army, perhaps with similar dramatic results. Arnim was not enthusiastic. The truth was that Rommel and Arnim were temperamentally antagonistic to one another if only because Arnim

Below: Although Bizerta was not captured by the Allies until May its harbor was often attacked to stop Rommel's supplies.

Right: Rommel's airfields were often attacked and many vital transport aircraft destroyed like this Ju-52 (foreground).

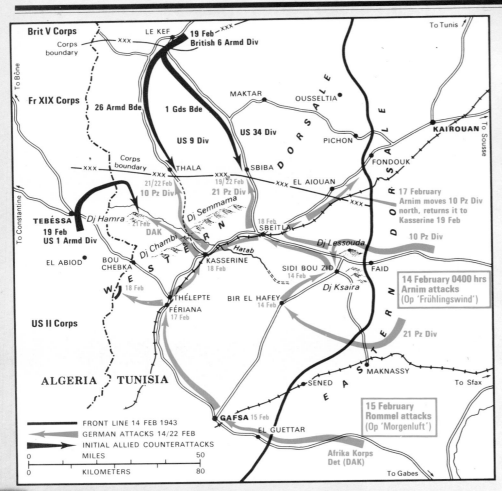

was a Prussian aristocrat. He was one of the chilly officers, 'the men of marble with cold, black hearts' whom Rommel had always despised and by whom he felt rejected. In any case, Fifth Panzer Army's commander took a totally different view of the war in Africa which he saw as a mere holding operation to tie down enemy forces and deny their use elsewhere. However, the proposal was referred to Commando Supremo and they agreed to it, largely through the mediation of Kesselring.

Almost immediately Rommel's mood underwent a total transformation. On 22 January he was writing disconsolately to Lucie; on the 25th he was 'so depressed he could hardly work.' Suddenly he was the old Rommel again, disposing his forces, bustling among them in his familiar leather overcoat to see his orders carried out, reprimanding any who failed to satisfy. The men themselves seemed to sense the alteration in him and greeted him joyously wherever he appeared among them.

On 12 February he celebrated two years in Africa. Very, very few of those who had come with him were still there; many had been killed and more had had to be moved for reasons of health. There was, however, a party in which 19 of the original contingent joined him.

Two days later the 21st Panzer Division, temporarily under Fifth Army, swept round the southern end of the Eastern Dorsale while the 10th Panzer Division broke through the pass at Faid and the two joined up at Sidi bou Zid. Behind them two American units comprising about 2000 men, rashly posted well forward on hills where they were incapable of mutual assistance, were bypassed and cut off. In the battle the Americans also lost 44 tanks and 26 guns. Outflanked and with Afrika Korps units threatening their tenuous front, II Corps

had to abandon the town of Gafsa and pull back to Fériana to the north. A counterattack to retake Sidi bou Zid failed with further heavy losses.

By the 17th Rommel was advancing on Fériana where, in preparation for withdrawal, massive demolitions were being carried out. In their panic, the Americans omitted to give the civilians the customary warning with the consequence that many were buried under the rubble of their own homes as explosions from fuel and ammunition dumps rocked the

Below: Men of the 2nd Battalion of the US 16th Infantry Regiment advance through the Kasserine Pass on 26 February.

town. The first task of the advancing German troops became that of digging out as many as possible of the survivors. However, 34 men, women and children died. In consequence, after only a few days of American occupation, the people greeted the Germans as liberators and Rommel himself was feted by local sheiks.

The battle continued, however, as one attacking force was sent northward toward Kasserine where a meeting with Fifth Army was to take place on the 18th and a second was turned westward toward Bou Chekba. Farther on lay Tebéssa and II Corps headquarters and behind that open country ideal for tanks. Fearful of being overrun, the American Corps commander ordered evacuation. In the process no attempt was made to maintain communication with units fighting in the south. The day also saw the fall of the key road junction of

Below: Both Rommel's forces and the Allies were hindered by the unpredictable winter weather in Tunisia.

Sbeitla to Arnim's troops. These were now themselves split, one battle group making for Kasserine and another north-westward to the pass at Sbiba.

Rommel at once saw what a victory might be gained if the attackers, taking advantage of American nervousness, seized Tebéssa with its airfield and used it as the springboard of an attack west-ward. He signalled Kesselring in Rome suggesting that with this in mind, he should mount an attack using his own 21st and Arnim's 10th Panzer Division. Kesselring agreed and Arnim was in-formed. Rommel knew that what he was attempting was fraught with danger, especially if the Anglo-American com-mand struck at his own long flank as he advanced and thereby cut off the attack-ing forces. He was reasonably con-vinced they would do no such thing. 'Commanders whose battles have so far all been fought in theory tend as a rule to react directly rather indirectly to the enemy's moves. Beginners generally lack the nerve to take decisions based on military expediency alone, without re-

gard for what is weighing most heavily on their minds,' he wrote later. He was as always a brilliant psychologist of the battlefield.

The initiative clearly lay with the German leaders for the moment but Rommel and Arnim could not agree on the next move. Rommel hoped to reach open country in the Allied rear after penetrating to Tebéssa but to achieve this he needed Arnim's 10th Panzer Division. Arnim wanted this unit for his own schemes.

The issue was sent to Commando Supremo for arbitration. They came down in favor of further offensive action, but, to Rommel's disappointment, want-ed it carried northward toward Le Kef, whereas he wanted to carry it in a more westerly direction through Tebéssa and then well beyond. In a more aggressively self-confident mood he would probably have gone his own way, dragging von Arnim in his train. As it was he gave these directives literal interpretation.

Behind the Allied front all was con-fusion and shock. Some Americans, who

had believed that Allied failures were solely due to British lack of dynamism, a weakness their own forces were about to redress, were among the first to panic when struck by Rommel's veterans. After the initial disasters Eisenhower had, on the suggestion of Churchill, appointed General Alexander to take charge of all land operations in North Africa under a new 18 Army Group headquarters. One of Alexander's first actions was to order that there was to be no further retreat beyond the Western Dorsale. The passes at Sbiba and Kasserine were to be held. In the meantime a British Guards Brigade had been stationed behind Sbiba to act in concert with the French and American forces already there. In attacks between 19–22 February, Rommel's 21st Panzers made little progress in this area.

However, at Kasserine things were far from satisfactory. The approaches were seized while Afrika Korps units made a feint at Tebéssa, the Nebelwerfer rocket-launchers being used for the first time in North Africa and proving extremely effective weapons. For a space it looked as if this attack, intended as a feint, would itself lead to a major victory but the German thrusts were stopped by American and French troops under US command. Another pass at Thala was successfully blocked by a British armored brigade and these minor successes gave the defenders time to increase their strength all along the line.

At this point, through a characteristic subterfuge, Rommel almost turned the whole tide of the battle in his own favor. Led by a captured British Valentine tank, his forces drove right through the defenses across the Thala road and the entire column was well into the Allied rear areas before it was recognized. In the two-hour battle which ensued, the Panzers were finally pushed back, but the cost to the Allied forces had been exorbitant and the defensive line so thinned that a determined push would have gone through it like a fist through wet tissue. It seemed impossible to avoid further withdrawals to consolidate.

At this low point in Allied fortunes the situation was saved by the outstanding performance of one Allied unit. This American artillery unit, under Brigadier General LeRoy Irwin, had disembarked at Algiers four days earlier. Told of the crucial struggle in progress, he and his men drove nonstop to Thala reaching it and positioning their guns during the night of the 22nd. They opened fire immediately and the impression of vast reinforcement their arrival gave completely discouraged Rommel. He was, in any case, growing anxious about the possibility of an attack on his Mareth positions which Montgomery had now reached. He decided to call off the battle. The operation had cost 10,000 Allies casualties of which 6500 were from II Corps alone. Axis losses were a mere 2000.

For the Americans it was a defeat of a magnitude rare in their history but in the

Below: Men of the Afrika Korps manhandle a 50mm antitank into a firing position. Few roads in Tunisia were as good as this.

Above: Meal time in a USAAF camp in Tunisia. American strategic bomber forces were built up in Africa to attack southern Europe.

long term its effects were probably beneficial in that they produced a greater comprehension on the American side of what their Allies had been up against. Indeed, from that time on the two sides worked with a sense of common purpose seldom found in the history of wartime coalitions. On the German side Rommel blamed failure on Arnim's lack of co-operation. Not only had Arnim for a time refused to allow his 10th Panzer Division to fight under Rommel's command, but also at another point when Rommel had asked for 19 Tiger tanks, then with Fifth Army, which he wanted to exploit his breakthrough at Thala, these too were refused.

However, Rommel was growing sicker by the day and at least some of his irritation with those around him must be attributed to this. By mid-February his personal physician, Professor Horster, regarded his condition as so serious that he declared nothing less than an immediate eight-week course of treatment in Europe was appropriate and that this

Right: A German infantryman checks his watch as he and his companions wait to go over the top into the attack.

should be started no later than the 20th. Measures for his departure from North Africa had actually begun, but were interrupted by the battle and the early successes of this had so startling a recuperative effect that Horster had agreed to a delay. The disappointing outcome of the battle brought about a relapse.

On the 22nd Kesselring asked Rommel if he would be prepared, despite his condition, to take command of an army group consisting of his own forces, now described as First Italian Army, and Fifth Panzer Army, a clear indication his reputation in Berlin remained high. He declined. Nonetheless, on the 23rd the appointment was made in a Commando Supremo order and, flatteringly, the new formation was given the title Army Group Rommel.

His direct concern, now the battle in northern Tunisia was over, was with Montgomery and the Mareth Line. He believed his only chance was to strike before the enemy had built up full strength and to do so he cancelled all arrangements for his return to Germany for treatment. On 6 March the Battle of Medenine began. At first it looked promising. The Nebelwerfer rocket launchers opened up in 90th Light's sector and

then 10th Panzer Division began the advance. Montgomery was ready. When the attackers were judged to be in the right position the skillfully disposed British artillery opened fire. By the evening Rommel had lost a third of his tanks and made no progress. The attack had to be called off.

Rommel was to some extent ready for such an outcome, and it played into his hands, for as early as the end of February he had asked von Arnim and Messe, now commanding First Italian Army, to draw up a full appreciation of the North African situation. As a result of this he requested formal permission to reduce his front from its present 400 miles to 100 by strategic withdrawals. Despite the defeat at Medenine, Hitler refused to countenance this. On 9 March Rommel decided to present his case for withdrawal personally to Commando Supremo in Rome, but though he finally reached Mussolini himself, he found a total lack of realism at every level in the Italian capital and it was also plain that the Italians regarded him as a broken reed, no longer fit for command and did not anticipate his return to Africa.

Next day Rommel was at Hitler's secret headquarters in the Ukraine.

Above: The end in Africa. Dejected German and Italian prisoners of war await transportation to proper camps.

There he argued not just for reducing the Axis front but for evacuating North Africa entirely and employing the troops thus made available for the defense of Italy which, he was convinced, would soon be invaded by the Allies. Hitler, was unconvinced, to say the least, and ordered Rommel to go on his delayed sick leave. Yet, even then, one oblique compliment was paid to him. It was ordered that every possible precaution should be taken to prevent the Allies from getting to know that he had left Africa. His reputation was still worth a division to the Axis.

On 6 May the end he had predicted came about. The British Eighth Army and the Anglo-American First Army combined to squeeze the Axis forces into a tiny bridgehead. By the 13th, with Tunis and Bizerta in Allied hands, the last Axis troops had been compelled to surrender. The Allies claimed to have taken 250,000 prisoners and though this is usually discounted by later more sober assessments, the number certainly exceeded those taken at Stalingrad.

8: ITALY AND FRANCE

The disillusionment Rommel felt with the German political system was beginning to reveal itself quite obviously by this time. He was, of course, ill. He had driven a difficult course between the Scylla of his direct superiors in Berlin and the Charybdis of Commando Supremo. He believed himself let down and misunderstood by both.

In mid-March 1943 he learned that he was not to return to Africa and this must certainly have been a bitter blow; for all that he felt it a lost cause. The thought of the men he had led and for whom he felt so close an affinity and affection ending their military careers in prisoner-of-war camps was, we know from his letters, a cause of deep sorrow, though later he was to be glad they were spared a worse fate in the final death throes of National Socialism.

In May 1943 Rommel's son Manfred, just in his teens, was called up. In a letter to Lucie dated 24 May, his father wrote, 'I can't get used to the idea yet that this 14-and-a-half-year old lad will be in barracks in a few months.' Later that year Manfred said he wanted to join the Waffen-SS and asked his father's permission. To his surprise it was not forthcoming. His father fully recognized the fighting qualities of the SS troops but did not want his son under the command of a man directly responsible for mass murder, by which he meant Heinrich Himmler. Even so Rommel still preferred to believe that Hitler was not party to what was going on. It was not until the following year that he realized his Führer was far from being innocent of it.

Militarily, Italy was now in the forefront. On 9 July Allied forces landed in Sicily and encountered little Italian resistance, though there were strong forces in the island. There was, however, stiff opposition from the Germans. Nonetheless, OKH believed that the Sicilian landings were a feint and that the real blow would come in Greece. This was the result of a successful British deception whereby fake Allied plans were

Left: A Priest 105mm self-propelled gun moves along a dusty Italian road. Rommel's forces first encountered these weapons at Alamein.

slipped into the possession of the Germans by way of their friends in Franco's Spanish government. As a result, Rommel, now restored to health, was made Commander in Chief, Southeast, a command which was to cover both Greece and Italy. On 23 July, after a hurried meeting with Hitler at the Wolf's Lair, he was sent to Salonika. His task was to make sure the German forces there were in a proper condition to face the anticipated assault.

While Rommel was engaged in this task a fresh blow fell. A coup d'état in Rome resulted in the fall of Mussolini and his replacement by Marshal Badoglio. The former dictator was taken into protective custody. Rommel, as well as many others, believed that the Badoglio regime's first act would be to try to conclude an armistice with the Allies and that if this happened it would place the enemy at Germany's back door.

On 26 July Rommel was back at Rastenburg for a conference whose importance is indicated by the fact that those present included not only army, navy and air force chiefs, but also party and government leaders, among them Foreign Minister von Ribbentrop, Reichsführer-SS Himmler, and Propaganda Minister Goebbels. Early Allied landings in Italy were expected and the Italian response was still unclear, though they were loudly protesting their loyalty to the Axis. Rommel, supported by others, wanted to march into Italy at once, but this action was delayed for political reasons. However, when it was known that secret negotiations with the Allies were in train, it was decided to seize the Brenner Pass. By 6 August it was felt that no further time could be lost and the Germans began pouring across the borders, sometimes encountering Italian resistance, but more often entering unopposed.

It was Rommel's view that the Allies, with their considerable amphibious capability, would probably land in the north of the Italian peninsula and he therefore argued that the Axis forces should make their main stand along well-fortified lines in this area. Kesselring, however, was opposed to this and believed it was pos-

Above: Admiral Hewitt, General Patton and Navy Secretary Knox. Hewitt and Patton both held commands during the invasion of Sicily.

Right: An MP ducks because of a nearby shell hit as a landing craft from the attack transport *James O'Hare* unloads at Salerno.

resistance there was came from German units who, only hours before, had taken over the coastal defenses.

Even after this, it was supposed that the main Allied effort would be in the form of landings farther north. It was some time before the Germans could accustom themselves to believe that their opponents had committed the monumental error of giving themselves the task of fighting their way up the entire peninsula which, with its rivers and mountain-chains, was eminently suited to defense. The struggle would occupy the Allies to the end of the war and cost many lives.

In the meantime, however, Rommel had fallen ill again, this time with a troublesome appendix which was speedily removed without complication. For a time Rommel was considered for the position of Supreme Commander in Italy, but his reputation for defeatism and pessimism finally prevented his appointment and on 21 November he was recalled to Germany.

Rommel might seem to be a defeatist to those who wanted only to hear the good news, but it should not be assumed

sible to stand south of Rome and deny the city to the Allies. On 3 September, though at the time it was unknown to the Germans, the Badoglio government signed the surrender and on the 8th the Allies began landing at Salerno. The surrender was announced just before they came ashore so as to prevent the Italian troops resisting. In fact, the only

Below: US troops practice landing operations. Rommel knew that such meticulous preparations could only be met by elaborate defenses.

Above: General Mark Clark commanded Fifth Army, of British and US troops, which made the landings at Salerno.

that this meant he had lost all hope for Germany. Though he doubted that Germany could win the war, he still believed that if the right measures were taken, a tolerable peace might be patched up. He believed that Germany now had to fight a defensive war, holding back the enemy by all possible means and building up her offensive capability until she was in a position to strike back. In a conversation with his former Chief of Staff,

Lieutenant General Fritz Bayerlein in July 1943, he explained these views in detail. The German war effort should be given over to producing the weapons of defense in enormous quantities. Deep defensive belts would shield Germany's borders in the east, and in the west the French coast would be fortified so that an Allied invasion would be both costly and in vain. If Rommel entertained doubts about the nation's leadership it was that they would fail to understand these imperatives and squander a vast proportion of the productive capacity on secret weapons whose ability to change the course of the war was uncertain.

However, in November 1943 it looked as if his ideas in at least one sphere were likely to be realized. He was sent on a tour of the Atlantic coastal defenses stretching from Denmark down to the Spanish frontier. By 15 December he was installed in France living in a chateau at Fontainebleau which, as he

Below: Rommel inspects defenses in Denmark during his review of the Atlantic fortifications in November 1943.

proudly told Lucie, had once belonged to Madame de Pompadour. Here he was able to take up riding again and the life of a country gentleman he enjoyed in his sparetime was rendered more complete by a present from the Todt Organization, the Third Reich's slave-masters, two dachshunds, one of which he gave to Lucie, and then a hunting dog. He set up his headquarters at La Roche Guyon in Normandy.

On the last day of December 1943 he reported back to Hitler. The invasion attempt would, he suggested, be made in the Pas de Calais area since it offered the shortest sea route and the closest access to the French ports needed to bring supplies ashore. He also thought it was likely that an early drive would be made to capture the launching sites for the new flying bombs and rockets which were shortly to be launched against Britain in a second Blitz.

Heavy bombing from the air and sea was to be anticipated as a prelude to invasion and this would probably itself be preceded by air drops intended to take the defenses in rear. The coastal line

was far too thinly held at present, he claimed, and this made it likely that the enemy would succeed in forming several bridgeheads with amphibious and airborne forces linking up. His recommended countermeasures were more or less those he had discussed with Bayerlein: deep belts of obstacles running from well inland down into the sea, altogether five or six miles in length. Within these would be interlocking fortified zones and the ultimate objective would be to destroy the enemy before he established himself ashore. His plans were grandiose, calling for the laying of some 200,000,000 mines in addition to foreshore obstacles, themselves mined, as well as an elaborate system of traps and mines against airborne forces, especially gliders.

These proposals were set in train and the months passed. By May some 6,000,000 mines had been sown and 517,000 of his foreshore obstacles stuck up from the low-tide mark. It was a far cry from the projected numbers, but no small achievement all the same. The preparations were mainly in the Pas de

Above: Rommel himself made these rough sketches of how the defenses should be prepared and operated.

to have his own ideas about how the coming battle should be fought and disposed his units accordingly. Erich Marcks, commanding 85th Corps, expected landings in his own area – Normandy or Brittany – and dismissed Rommel's early arguments that the rocky coastline there would dissuade the Allied planners. Geyr von Schweppenburg, commanding 86th Corps, had a plan for holding his Panzer forces as far back as Paris on the grounds that an Allied offensive would have this as its major objective and he wanted to be in a position to meet them on ground of his own choosing. Rommel still held to his conviction that the invaders would have to be defeated on the beaches and that the beaches in question were most likely to be those in the Pas de Calais area.

This confusion about the chosen point for landings, indeed whether the Allies intended to land at all, was being actively fostered by an extensive deception apparatus. The extent to which this succeeded is shown by the fact that though Rommel's defensive obstacles had sprung up all along the European seaboard, their main concentration was opposite the southeastern coast of Britain. Rommel himself was as tireless as ever, not only in creating his great *chevaux de frise*, but also in trying to improve the combat readiness of the troops who, he felt, had

Below: Field Marshal von Rundstedt joins in the round of inspections. He is shown here leaving an artillery bunker.

Calais area but Rommel was now becoming concerned that the landings might be made further west, in Normandy or Brittany, with the great port of Cherbourg as their objective and he tried with all possible haste to get the stretches of coast in both places equally well fortified. He was, at the same time, jockeying to get control of all forces in the area, arguing that it was essential to success in the coming battle that they were under unified command.

Although ambition undoubtedly played a significant part in this, it was also dictated by sheer logic. Technically, he was subordinate to the Commander in Chief, West, the 68 year old Field Marshal von Rundstedt and beyond this

to OKW. This meant he was in a position only to recommend and not to direct. Rundstedt, an able and cunning strategist, age notwithstanding, had to a very great extent abandoned all hope of defeating an Allied invasion, an attitude inevitably affecting the enthusiasm with which Rommel's plans for defense were carried out.

However, on 15 January 1944 Rommel was given command of the German armies along the sector from the Loire to Holland, including the occupation troops in that country. These forces, the Fifteenth and Seventh Armies, were effectively those facing Britain and so likely to be in the forefront of the fighting against any landings.

In fact, even within this organization there was a fundamental lack of coordination, largely because every German general in western Europe seemed been living a soft life for too long and had lost stomach for the fight.

In late February Rommel flew home on leave. Lucie was living in a villa at Herrlingen and there they were visited by a certain Dr Karl Strölin, Mayor of Stuttgart (the office which, by a quirk of fate, Manfred Rommel now occupies). The doctor had been making preparations for this meeting for weeks offering gifts and flattery to Frau Rommel to bring it about. The purpose was to drag her husband into an anti-Hitler plot.

Below: Rommel and Engineer General Meise test beach defenses. Such obstacles, often mined, would hinder landing craft at high tide.

Above: Field Marshal Rommel and his wife and son. The Rommels had a very happy marriage.

According to David Irving, Strölin got short shrift. Rommel shut him up in the middle of his account of atrocities in the east and sent him packing. The field marshal's mood of deep pessimism had given place to confidence about the forthcoming battle, seeing in it fresh chances for glory he was hardly likely to want to throw away in a dangerous political gamble. In any case, he may well have been alarmed by Strölin's openness in expressing views which could have incriminated not only himself but Lucie and Manfred as well.

Back at Fontainebleau in early March, Rommel was presented with a document which amounted to a fresh oath of allegiance to his Führer. Like most other commanders who were confronted with it, he signed without demur.

Through this period, Rommel's views about where the invasion was to take place underwent some change largely as a result of a similar change of view by Hitler who had become convinced it would be in the Brittany–Normandy region. At a meeting of generals from the west in mid-March, the Führer developed this theme, adding that when it came, the invasion force was to be destroyed within hours, at most within days. Once this had been done, the 43 German divisions in the west could be dispatched east to transform the situation there. This was a supremely optimistic reading of events. Nonetheless, Rommel, whose own changed mood we have already noted, seemed to gain further encouragement from it.

The next six weeks saw him once more back at work driving from one end of the coast to the other. There was, however, another incident, small in itself, which was to have later consequences. Rommel was sent a new Chief of Staff, General Hans Speidel. Besides being an able soldier, Speidel was also a historian and something of a musician. The two men took to each other instantly. Speidel, unknown to his new chief, was deeply implicated in the anti-Hitler conspiracy and had actually had a meeting with Strölin the day before he took up his duties in France. Almost certainly the conspirators within the army hoped that Speidel would win Rommel over to their cause.

It was a more difficult task than they had apparently realized. In May Rommel had written to Manfred declaring that British morale was at break point. Strikes were endemic. Demonstrators on the streets were calling, 'Down with Churchill and the Jews.' It all sounded more like a leader in *Völkischer Beobachter* than the statements of a man about to help in pulling the government down.

Information fed to the German commanders by the British continued to suggest that the invasion was to be in the Pas de Calais – Hitler alone was skeptical – and that it would come in May. In the meantime, all round Rommel the plotters were at their stealthy work, the tentacles of their intrigues stretching as far as Paris where the commandant, General von Stülpnagel, had become involved. There was still no evidence that Rommel was himself implicated nor even that any real attempt had been made to recruit him.

On 2 June 1944 Rommel went to Paris where he bought a pair of shoes to give to Lucie as a birthday present on the 6th. By the 4th he was back in Germany, intending to celebrate the birthday and then visit Hitler.

Expectation of invasion had been sustained for so long that it had begun to lose its edge. Some German officers went so far as to express the view that it had already been left too late to be practicable. To establish firm bridgeheads the Allies would need the entire summer and ought, therefore, to have invaded in the spring.

Forty-eight hours after his arrival at Herrlingen, the German navy declared that the seas were too rough for their patrol vessels to put to sea. So it was that the Allied invasion fleet, numbering nearly 6500 vessels, crossed unopposed and began to disgorge their troops at those very places along the French northwest coast that Hitler had suspected – the Normandy beaches. Allied paratroops had landed in the German rear to seize bridges and road junctions and prevent the movement of reinforcements, as Rommel forecast they would. Though in places domination of the beaches was contested through the whole day, by evening all the assault troops had begun to move inland. Confusion on the German part was con-founded by the belief, again fostered by the Allies, that this was a feint and that the real thing was still to come in the Pas de Calais.

Thus, as at Alamein, Rommel was away from the crucial front when the long-expected attack came. He learned of events only by way of a telephone call from Speidel. The beach obstacles had had little effect, he was told. For the most part they were destroyed by groups of sappers landed in advance of the invaders. The landings were actually made at low tide, avoiding the most formidable

Below: Rommel is pictured outside a typical artillery emplacement on the Brittany coast.

obstacles and not at high tide, as Rommel
had confidently expected. Worse still
Rommel discovered, when he reached
his headquarters late that night, no
counterattack had been undertaken, because the Panzers were being held for
the expected real assault to the east. It
was 10 hours before the units were released and they then had to drive west.
It was weeks before the German commanders ceased to be convinced that the
true invasion was yet to come.

From the point of view of the attackers,
we know that the ensuing days and weeks
were full of frustration with their time-
table being badly dislocated. The bocage
country of Normandy with its many
small fields and narrow lanes flanked by
high hedgerows, lent itself to defense
against armor. Tanks or antitank guns
lurking in ambush could halt an entire
advance by destroying the lead vehicle of
an Allied column. The brunt of the
fighting therefore fell upon the hapless
Allied infantry, who were forced to
eliminate the enemy strongpoints one by
one.

While the American forces on the
Allied left were gathering for a break out
attack, the British Second Army under
Rommel's old opponent, Bernard Mont-

Below: A burning infantry landing craft
off Omaha beach. Rommel's beach
defenses nearly worked here.

Above: Rommel's opponents in Normandy. From left, General Hodges, Field Marshal Montgomery, Generals Bradley and Dempsey.

gomery, was fighting to capture the ancient university city of Caen with the intention of drawing as much as possible of the German tank force away from the Americans, an endeavor in which they were highly successful. The battle was to prove a long and bloody one, however, with the inhabitants of the city and its famous buildings among the first casualties.

If the Allied commanders were concerned about slowed-down timetables, from the opposite side of the lines the battle looked even less promising, as the Germans began to realize the attackers' quantitative superiority in material of war. The principal worry was Cher-

bourg, since not only Hitler, but also his generals were convinced that the key to Allied success lay in the early capture of a port for landing supplies and reinforcements. They were, of course, arguing without taking into consideration Allied ingenuity. The Allies had prepared against the possibility of failure to seize a port by building prefabricated harbors which they simply towed across the Channel, while the beachmasters had become such experts in their trade that it proved possible to land supplies on the open beaches throughout the summer. Progress was never impeded for lack of supplies.

Rommel, meanwhile, spent the days following his return to Normandy in chasing up and down the fighting line. The optimism of only a few days before gave way to a growing desperation, es-

pecially in view of Allied air superiority. There was still no sign he was about to throw in his lot with the anti-Hitler plotters who seemed, more than ever, convinced that Germany's sole salvation lay in substituting Rommel as head of a caretaker government, an opinion not actually communicated to the man himself, or, if communicated, done so in terms so oblique he does not appear to have understood. Their only point of contact with one another was that he shared their belief that peace must be made with the west in order that the struggle in the east could go on.

On 12 June Hitler gave a totally unrealistic order for a counterattack which was to throw the invaders back into the sea. It got nowhere, failing even to recapture the town of Carentan, a subsidiary objective, recently fallen to the

Left: American paratroops advance near Carentan on 14 June. They are on the look out for snipers.

Americans. Hitler, however, had now extended his no-retreat policy to France and refused to countenance the withdrawals which alone would have allowed the regrouping and concentration of the defenders and hence their employment at full strength. Such orders as this were, not unnaturally, affecting Rommel's own psychology and making him easier prey to the whisperings of the plotters, though their tacit agreement about the way the war ought to be ended remained the limit of his sympathies.

On 17 June Hitler himself arrived in France. Under a barrage of arguments from his commanders, he agreed to some modification of the no-retreat order as far as the Cherbourg Peninsula was concerned so that maximum force could be concentrated in defense of the port

Below: The scene on the beaches and offshore as the Allied buildup proceeds. Allied air power made the barrage balloons unnecessary.

itself. At the same time he told them that the flying-bomb attacks against Britain had begun and presented a highly exaggerated report of the damage done materially and morally. Rommel at one point ventured to suggest that the time was approaching when political moves would have to supersede military initia-

tives. He received a curt order to mind his own business. Yet, even after this snub, Rommel seems to have left the meeting with all his pro-Hitler sentiments revived and even in a certain buoyancy of mood.

On the 18th the Americans linked up across the Cherbourg peninsula and the troops in the port were cut off. Everyone, Rommel included, knew its days were numbered. It was not actually until 29

July, that Cherbourg was indisputably in Allied hands. Its capture cost them 20,000 lives, while German losses were about double that number. So thoroughly had the demolition engineers done their work, however, that it was weeks before the port could be brought back into use, and this was wholly due to the energetic efficiency of the American engineers.

The day before Cherbourg fell Rommel was on his way back to the Berghof, Hitler's country retreat in south Germany. He went determined to speak his mind and found an ally in the Commander in Chief, West, Gerd von Rundstedt. All the same he hardly expected a sympathetic hearing and had actually gone to the length of arranging a brief meeting with Lucie and Manfred beforehand in case he was arrested.

It is certainly true that by the time of the meeting the confidence of a fortnight earlier had largely been dissipated. The defenders of Germany's eastern frontier were being remorselessly pushed backward by Soviet armor. There was still the struggle going on in the bocage, but the Allies were building up their

Above: British-manned Sherman tanks pass through Reviers in Normandy. An unarmed command tank is in the lead.

Below: As in his other campaigns Rommel tried to get close to the front to discuss the situation with local commanders.

strength and might at any time break out. All the same, Rommel was shouted down when he tried to deploy his arguments for seeking peace. When he persisted he was ordered by Hitler to leave the room. Thus ended what was in fact his last meeting with his Führer.

Whatever further blows he anticipated from an angry Hitler did not fall and as it happened it was von Rundstedt who was compelled to resign, the excuse being his age. Rommel, who expected to be promoted in Rundstedt's place was deeply shocked when instead a general from the Eastern Front, Field Marshal von Kluge, was appointed. In a rancorous first interview, Kluge angered Rommel by telling him that the time had come when he too must learn to obey orders. In particular, he was prohibited from making direct appeals to Hitler, though he continued to do so.

The two men had already met in France in 1940, where Kluge was superior to Rommel. Although Kluge gave 'complete approval' to plans submitted to him by Rommel during the Battle of France, there seems to have been a certain coolness between the two of them. When Rommel invited him to write a foreword to a manuscript, on the French campaign he was preparing, Kluge pointed out some of the exaggerations in which the former 7th Division commander had indulged. Kluge also seems to have accepted the analysis made by OKH that Rommel was an irredeemable pessimist, though he himself realized there was little cause to be otherwise when he had toured his new command.

Nowhere was the heroic resistance of German troops, many of them hardly more than children, doing more than slow down the Allies grinding advance.

Above: German troops surrender in a town in northern France as the Allied advance continues.

Below: An American M 24 tank moves along a street littered with victims of Allied air power – dead horses and burned trucks.

Into the bargain there was still the belief in further landings. David Irving claims to read into this the machinations of Rommel's staff with their deep-laid plots. This is, of course, to ignore many of the facts which were influencing German calculations. There was to begin with the elaborate and sustained program of deception, as well as the mystery of why one of the most brilliant of the Allied commanders, George Patton, had failed to appear on the battlefield. Lastly, there was the alarming fact that whatever resources of infantry the enemy might or might not still have at his disposal, there was no doubt that he had in Britain a considerable airborne force, the Allied First Airborne Army made up of Polish, American and British units, which had been unemployed since the preinvasion drops. The fact that Eisenhower had at that moment no precise plans for their use did not in any way diminish the fear their existence aroused.

9:THE IMPLACABLE FATE

Discounting the day-to-day tasks of command, which continued to take an enormous emotional toll of Rommel's failing strength since he was trying to run a battle against overwhelming odds with little support and indeed much hindrance from above, Rommel appears at this time as a man in the midst of a terrible conflict: to believe or abandon belief in Hitler. That he was at no time privy to an assassination attempt we can accept with confidence, not only from our knowledge of his character, but also on the basis of reports of his conversation before and after the plot to kill Hitler.

While on the one hand he was disgusted at the constant alterations to his own plans by those miles from the battlefront and the refusal to see that withdrawal could sometimes be a strategic necessity, he seems to have blamed this state of affairs more on the men around Hitler than on the man himself. On the other hand he could see with his own eyes, and his belief was corroborated by others, that fundamental political decisions had to be made quickly. He persisted in the conviction that Hitler would sooner or later reach a similar conclusion and it is indicative of a vast political naivety that he actually supposed the Western Allies could be persuaded to involve themselves in a new war with Germany and against the Soviet Union, totally ignoring the fact that it had been Germany which invaded the USSR and not vice versa so that to Western minds justice was firmly on the side of the Red Army.

In July 1944 the plotters, who had been wooing Rommel ceaselessly, were fast approaching the time of irrevocable action. They, therefore, sent Caesar von Hofacker, a colonel in the Luftwaffe, to Rommel. He showed as little sympathy as he had shown other visitors with similar missions and it seems certain

Left: Scenes of rejoicing in a French town. The operations of the resistance and their many supporters disrupted Rommel's plans.

there was no mention of assassination. All the same, Hofacker left under the impression that the field marshal had been won over entirely and reported this belief to his accomplices. Rommel was now openly mentioned as the chosen head of a future, post-Hitler government which was to treat with the west. Another step had been taken toward the fate which was to overcome him.

Rommel was actually to play into its hands by his own candor. In the battles since the Allied landings he had lost approaching 100,000 men and had had only 6000 replacements. His 225 lost tanks had been replaced by a mere 17. On 15 July a report was drafted in which such statistics as well as the alarming situation generally were outlined. Appending his signature thereto, Rommel imprudently added a conclusion stating: 'The unequal struggle is drawing to its close. In my view the political consequences of this should be drawn.' The next day, visiting the front, the question of the future course of the war was raised during a chance meeting with an officer who had served on Rommel's staff in North Africa. Rommel told him, 'Field Marshal Kluge and I have sent an ultimatum to the Führer telling him the war cannot go on militarily.' He was asked what happened if the Führer did not agree? 'Then I am going to open up the Western Front, because the only thing that matters now is that the British and Americans get to Berlin before the Russians,' he answered.

Still another twist was yet to come. In July a British Special Air Service squad was dropped behind the German lines with the mission of either kidnapping or killing the German general. This, of course, was not the first such attempt; there had been the Keyes' Raid in North Africa. It is, on the other hand, difficult to understand its purpose now Rommel's name no longer exerted its magic spell and, with their own superiority, the Allies had no need to fear him for himself. In any event, the enterprise miscarried simply because Rommel was not

Left: Field Marshal von Kluge (right) was Rommel's superior in France. He committed suicide after the attempt on Hitler's life.

to be found. The reason was that, unknown to the SAS squad, he was at death's door in hospital.

On 17 July Rommel visited the headquarters of General 'Sepp' Dietrich, commander of the I SS Panzer Corps. Its ostensible purpose was to discuss an attack expected from Montgomery's Second Army, but it also touched on the war at large and its ending. Rommel told his aide, Captain Helmuth von Lang as they left that he had 'won Dietrich over.' They drove back through roads congested with the jetsam of war of which the most pitiable were the French, refugees for the second time in four years.

Approaching the little town of Livarot, a lookout spotted enemy aircraft. The driver swerved off the main road into a lane but had not gone far before he was back on the wide Route Nationale once more. The aircraft spotted them and swooped down with cannons firing, the attack, it was suggested later, being a sort of airborne attempt to do what the SAS had failed in, though there is no real evidence for this. Both Rommel and his driver were hit. The car went out of control and rushed down the hill to hit a tree and throw its passengers out.

Lang, who was more or less unhurt, went in search of another car to convey the wounded to hospital and took 45 minutes in the task. They were first taken to a French religious hospital nearby where the surgeon, after examining Rommel's injuries, pronounced him unlikely to recover. Later he was moved, still unconscious, to a Luftwaffe hospital 25 miles away. His driver, who accompanied him, died during the night. After emergency treatment and three days' rest, the field marshal was transferred to yet another hospital, at Vesinet near St Germain where the highly skilled Professor Esch was in charge, and it was to him that Rommel probably owed his life. In the meantime, news of what had happened reached the Commander in Chief, West, von Kluge, and he took over personal command of Rommel's army

Left: Himmler (left) and SS General Dietrich. Rommel conferred with Dietrich on 17 July before he was wounded.

Above: Hitler and Mussolini inspect the damaged conference room at Hitler's HQ after the bomb plot.

group.

On 20 July, while Rommel was still unconscious, Hitler attended a staff conference at Rastenburg. The first man to arrive was Colonel Claus von Stauffenberg who left shortly after it began, apparently forgetting a briefcase he had left on the floor propped against one leg of a heavy map table. In it was enough explosive material, attached to a timing device, to wipe out everyone in the room.

During the ensuing discussion, one of the participants tripped on it and kicked it farther under the table. When it exploded, as it duly did, much of the force of the blast was absorbed by the table. Three men were killed and two others were badly injured. The Führer himself escaped with no more than burns and lacerations.

What followed was a witch hunt as hideous as any in Nazi history, rivalling even those with which medieval kings pursued regicides. Stülpnagel made an abortive attempt at suicide; Kluge, on the periphery of the plot, made a successful one, and he was only one of many. Hundreds, among them some of Germany's most distinguished soldiers, were rounded up, some summarily executed, others tortured, questioned and arraigned before an army court of honor. When they were stripped of rank and discharged, they were handed over to the tender mercies of the People's Court under the National Socialist Robespierre,

Roland Freisler. Several thousand died, many in the most grotesque and barbaric circumstances.

Rommel, we know, had had no part in the assassination attempt. One of his first actions on recovering consciousness and learning of it was to condemn it and, in an early letter to Lucie, dictated from his bed he wrote, 'Coming on top of my accident, the attempt on the Führer's life has given me a terrible shock.' He continued to denounce it, not only because of its inherent criminality, but also because of its imprudence.

However, among those who had fallen

Below: Especially after 20 July Hitler kept portraits of Frederick the Great – a German leader who won through from adversity.

into Gestapo hands was von Hofacker, who had been convinced after the earlier meeting that Rommel was on the plotters' side at least as far as replacing Hitler was concerned. Under questioning he opened up, profligately naming names, Rommel's among them. One would be wrong to ascribe this to cowardice. It is far more likely it formed part of some scheme of his own perhaps to demonstrate that the opposition to Hitler was more widespread than had been supposed and thereby sow a general distrust in the armed forces and its command. No doubt, too, he felt that Rommel's reputation was enough to protect him from even Hitler's wrath. At least to begin with, this was true. The Führer was at first placatory, talking of retiring Rommel and leaving matters there.

While the investigation was at its height the injured man was making what all regarded as a miraculous recovery, defying medical opinion. He was soon talking of getting back to the Normandy front and alarmed his doctors by his refusal to stay in bed. On 1 August he even held a press conference in Paris to show that, contrary to Allied reports, he was still very much alive. On 8 August he was considered well enough to be moved to Germany and returned by car to the Herrlingen villa. Naturally, he was still in need of concentrated and intensive care, but doctors were available at the nearby University of Tübingen. At the same time Manfred was for a period seconded from his antiaircraft unit to his father's staff at home – the indication that he was still able to exact privileges. In this way the two of them came to know each other better perhaps than at any earlier time.

Rommel must have appreciated only too well that his open expressions of 'defeatist' opinion on the war meant he could hardly escape the Gestapo's attention in the present circumstances, and reports of mysterious prowlers round the house and village began to reach the family from neighbors. After this Rommel always went out armed and advised Manfred to do the same. It is probable he expected an attempt on his life. In view of his recent accident, this could be passed off as enemy action and could save embarrassment all round. He also seems to have thought the end would come from a sniper's bullet.

Among the innocent visitors to the villa was Speidel, himself arrested soon after on 7 September. Rommel, when he heard of this, immediately wrote to Hitler seeking his intervention, a letter which was his last to his leader and which may finally have sealed Rommel's fate. In any case, Hitler's feelings had changed. Investigations had revealed that the name of his once favorite field marshal had been canvassed as a future head of state. This was too much.

Below: Field Marshal von Rundstedt arrives to deliver the oration at Rommel's funeral.

Just a month later Rommel was ordered to Berlin for a conference and told that a special train was to be sent to fetch him from Ulm. He refused to go, believing it to be a ruse to arrest and perhaps secretly dispose of him. On 14 October Erwin and Lucie Rommel travelled to visit an old friend who had got into the Gestapo's bad books and expected arrest at any moment. He expressed the opinion that Rommel was himself so popular with the German people as to be impervious to Hitler's malice, a view the field marshal vehemently dismissed. They arrived home to be told that 'two generals' wanted to make an appointment to discuss Rommel's future employment. The meeting was fixed for midday next day.

The visitors arrived punctually, Manfred fearing that it was as likely that they had come to arrest his father as to offer him further command. Their courteous manner was some reassurance however.

They were ushered into the field marshal's study and after only a few moments of conversation he emerged, pale, and went upstairs to his wife's room. Manfred followed anxiously and they held a brief meeting on the landing at which his father told him the terrible choice just put before him.

He could elect to be tried by a People's Court on a charge of high treason and hope to establish his innocence, but if found guilty, risk not only a death sentence but being stripped of all his titles and having all his property confiscated by the state. This would leave his wife and son penniless. Alternatively, he could discreetly take his own life right away. This would be treated as a sudden, but natural death following his injuries and he would keep his titles and be buried with full military honors with his property passing normally to his family.

Of his choice and of his final act, little need be said. Manfred reports that his father left the house by car with the two officers. They drove to some suitably secluded spot and Rommel was there handed a phial of cyanide which he drained. Even so death did not come at once. The driver of the car, Heinrich Doose, was ordered to get out and walked along the road for some five to 10 minutes. When he returned Rommel was still alive, but in his death throes, his cap lying on the car floor. The same witness records that the only sign that he was in extremis was that he was sobbing.

In the meantime, mother and son, in desperate misery and suspense, awaited the news they knew would come. Within 20 minutes the telephone began ringing. It was a call from a local reserve hospital. The field marshal had had a brain seizure on his way to a conference and they were grieved to report his death therefrom. Those around Hitler kept their word. Frau Rommel was left in full possession

Below: Rommel's coffin is carried in procession. An officer walks in front bearing Rommel's baton and medals.

Left: Lucie Rommel and Manfred outside the Town Hall at Ulm during the funeral. Nazi Party dignitaries stand behind them.

of her husband's property and duly received a widow's pension from the state.

There was a special department of Goebbels' Propaganda Ministry responsible for state funerals. These occasions had always had a special significance to National Socialism with their tawdry revivals of Teutonic myths of the noble warrior going to his modern Valhalla. Goebbels' department had actually cut its teeth way back in the years of struggle when Goebbels designed (that is the only possible word) a magnificent and highly emotional send-off for Horst Wessel, a young SA thug shot by a Communist. That had been the beginning of hypocrisy, for the man who was to become the Nazis' protomartyr had actually drifted out of the party at the time of his death which itself had nothing to do with politics anyway and was over a girl. The propaganda department's assignment now was to plan the spectacular funeral of the man National Socialism had finally killed.

To few generals on either side has such an accretion of legend adhered as to Field Marshal Erwin Johannes Eugen Rommel, the son of the Heidenheim schoolmaster. Its foundations were, of course, laid in the Western Desert where he turned what seemed like inevitable defeat for the Axis forces into a run of stunning victories admired by the world. This turn of fortune was remarked on both sides and he was quickly christened the Desert Fox because he too seemed wily and sharp toothed. Auchinleck had to go to the length of instituting special measures to try to diminish the apprehension aroused by the mere name. Rommel represented something else besides military genius as far as his enemies were concerned. He was 'the decent German general.' From some points of view this was more damaging to the British cause than the successful German general. Propaganda was presenting the opposing military leadership as arrogant, brutal and humorless. Here was one who was the very opposite of these things, who possessed, one could say, the virtues the British admired: good manners, charm, chivalry and a sense of humor – and this was not missed by neutrals, either. It is instruc-

Above: Roosevelt and Churchill combined to thwart Rommel in his finest hour after the fall of Tobruk when extra supplies of Sherman tanks were sent to Egypt from the US.

tive that Rommel was only once portrayed in the wartime cinema. This was in a film made in the early days of the desert war and Erich von Stroheim, the stereotype of the unpleasant German officer was cast in the role. It was a manifest travesty so gross even by the standards of wartime propaganda that thereafter the film industry felt it more discreet not to revert to the subject.

The assessment of Rommel's military skill has been undertaken by many others and their general conclusions are that he was able, resourceful, good at managing men and at detecting and exploiting any weakness the enemy chanced to exhibit. His supreme gift was as military psychologist, judging situations and his opponents to a nicety. He was not the genius of the battlefield he is sometimes represented as being. On the contrary, he suffered from very considerable failings. In particular that one, so often found in self-made men, of never fully trusting subordinates to do their job competently. It was this which led to his 'popping up all over the battlefield' in Sir Basil Liddell-Hart's phrase, when he would have been better occupied at this own headquarters coordinating the entire operation. It was this same failing which

led him to blame others in moments of adversity.

What distinguishes Rommel from his British opponents is not genius but something more prosaic: sheer technical mastery of his trade imparted by a first class training which gave attention to every detail. It was this which made the German staff-officer the finest in the world and so formidable an opponent. Rommel's ultimate defeat is now generally and rightly recognized as having

more to do with the fact that he was not supplied with the material and reinforcement essential to him while Montgomery was. One can safely state that any of a very large number of German commanders, sent to North Africa, might have done as well or possibly better than Rommel did. One finds oneself compelled to agree with the view of him expressed by his Führer: 'I regard Rommel . . . as being an exceptionally bold and also a clever commander. But I don't regard him as a stayer.'

There was in him a manic-depressive aspect, swinging wildly from exultant, bombastic euphoria in success to dejection in reverses – a trait far from uncommon among German generals, incidentally. Where in others, like Ludendorff, this led to a loss of nerve on the battlefield, in Rommel it produced physical symptoms and he became ill.

This brings one to a more controversial aspect of his personality, his reputation as the 'decent German general.' Of course, he was a thoroughly likable human being, a good husband and father, a friend whose loyalty was such he was prepared to risk himself, as he did with Speidel, in time of trial. However, at this distance in history one can declare that there were many Germans

Below: A picture that sums up Rommel's generalship. He sits in his Storch ready to fly to the front to take charge.

who, while they served the nauseating Third Reich loyally and even belonged to the party itself, were perfectly decent, if deluded, human beings.

We know that Rommel destroyed the *Führerbefehl* directing that all captured British commandos should be summarily executed, that he treated Allied prisoners of war humanely and courteously, even accepting repeated escape attempts with resigned good humor. However, Rommel had no monopoly of such attitudes. Countless Jews owed their lives to the protection afforded them by the German army which recruited them for labor and insisted their labor was 'essential to the war effort' when the persecutors came. The employment of Jews by the army reached such proportions, indeed, that questions were asked by Himmler's creatures about officers' loyalty to the principles of National Socialist ideology. Other German commanders risked their lives in efforts to impede the efforts of the extermination squads.

Why then has Rommel been selected for canonization? The answer seems perfectly simple. In North Africa both British and Germans were fighting across territory which rightly belonged to others. Neither saw the other as an invader. In this lies the difference between the desert war and all the other campaigns of the German army. Had Rommel's activities been limited to his involvement in the French battles of 1940, undoubtedly he would have been seen as just another barbarous invader. In the

Below: A landmark in the final defeat of Germany. US troops captured the Rhine bridge at Remagen in March 1945.

desert he was no more nor less of an invader than the British themselves and because of this the two sides could regard each other dispassionately. All assessments of him are affected by this. Furthermore, while it suited Goebbels to have a photogenic, personable and moreover successful general for his purposes, there was also a certain perspective from which it suited British propaganda. It helped, of course, to show its objectivity, but what was more important it

Below: A Soviet Stalin tank in Berlin. Rommel argued that Germany should make peace in the west to prevent such an outcome.

helped, especially in the latter days, to show what happened to 'decent Germans' in Hitler's Third Reich. By murdering him, the Nazis helped to underline this lesson.

His death and its circumstances could easily raise him to the stature of a tragic hero. Yet in a strange way he fails in this respect. He seems just a little too self-certain. The true tragic hero needs more self-doubt, a great deal more humility. There is, too, an insurmountable obstacle. All our judgments of Germans of the time are conditioned by the answer to one question: what, in the end, was their attitude to Nazism? Right to the

last Rommel was ambivalent. In one way, Rundstedt was perfectly right to say he died with 'the Führer in his heart.'

For this to have happened something besides the political innocence and naivety attributed to him by overloyal admirers was needed. Politically innocent and naive soldiers were as common in Germany as they were – and still are – elsewhere, and while they played their role in bringing National Socialism to their country, they did not sign their letters 'Heil Hitler,' did not talk of a 'Jewish problem,' did not read and cite *Völkischer Beobachter* which even Hitler himself regarded as a comic. Many of

Above: The veterans of the Afrika Korps established this memorial to their former leader, for whom they had great respect.

them, early or late, came to recognize the Frankenstein monster they had helped to create. Some gave their lives in the effort to destroy it. Theirs was, truly, a tragic fate.

There was an element of the war which Rommel and other German generals totally overlooked. In Napoleon's analysis, the struggle may go to the one who has the biggest battalions, but there is a moral element as well, as Speidel in his book on the invasion of 1944 points out. It is not just empty piety to believe that justice lends strength to a cause. Equally, as reality

began to penetrate it had a perhaps even stronger opposite effect upon the Germans. In his constant complaints about failure to support him, Rommel seems to have lost sight of the fact that there were certainly times, especially in the later stages, when his officers and men were asking themselves, is what we are fighting and dying for worth the sacrifice?

To some this may all add up to a niggardly appraisal of one who has enjoyed such acclaim. It is hard to see how, keeping all the data in mind, one could come to any other.

One might conclude that Rommel was a highly gifted, sometimes inspired, German commander, who fully concurred in the ideals of chivalry cherished by European armies, his own included,

and which did have some effect in mitigating the horrors of war, even if an insufficient one. He leaves the impression of a simple, honest, likable, patriotic man – all virtues which are far from contemptible. Abstemious in every facet of life, his dullness and his lack of interest in the finer things was counterbalanced by a considerable sense of humor and not a little tolerance.

It might be going too far to suggest that he was not actually overintelligent, but at least it can be said that such intellectual gifts as he possessed and these included an unusually penetrating clarity of mind, were employed entirely in the service of his military vocation – an attitude encouraged by German officer-training of the time.

INDEX

ACKNOWLEDGEMENTS

The author would like to thank Laurence Bradbury, the designer, Richard Natkiel, who drew the maps, Ellen Crampton, who prepared the index and Donald Sommerville, the editor. The Bundesarchiv kindly supplied most of the illustrations and the remainder were provided by the agencies and individuals listed below.

Bayerische Hauptstaatsarchiv, Munich, 11
Bison Picture Library, 10 bottom, 12–13 bottom, 28, 31, 32–33, 34 top, 36, 75 top, 89 both top, 92 top left, mid left, center, 90–91 all, 94 top, 95 top, 144, 157 bottom.
ECPA, 12 top
Robert Hunt Library, 9 both, 10 top, 13 top, 15 top, 19, 54 top, 89 bottom, 92 top right, 118 top, 120 top and middle, 127 top, 143 top, 145 all, 147
Imperial War Museum, 1, 6, 7, 8, 14–15 bottom, 42–43 bottom, 44 top, 44–45 bottom, 48–49 bottom, 50, 52–53 all, 58, 60–61 bottom, 62 bottom, 70–71 bottom left, 80–81 both, 82–83, 84 bottom left, 87 top, 88, 97 top, 98 bottom, 101 top right, 106–107 bottom, 112 top, 113 bottom, 114, 118 bottom, 120–121 bottom, 121 top, 122 middle, 128 top, 129 both, 138 bottom, 139, 140, 146 top, 148 top, 149, 152 both, 153 bottom, 158, 159, 160, 162 bottom, 165
Kriegsarchiv, Vienna, 16
National Archives (US), 14 top
National Maritime Museum (UK), 132–133
Novosti, 164
Orbis, 23, 153 top

Popperfoto, 60
John Taylor, 94–95 bottom
US Air Force, 126 top, 138 top, 142–143 top
US Army, 96 all, 124, 126–127 bottom, 134–135, 142–143 bottom, 150 top, 163
US Coast Guard, 148 bottom
USIS, 154
US Navy, 92–93 bottom, 142 top, 150–151 bottom, 162 top